Getting Away With Murder

Getting Away With Murder

HOW POLITICS IS DESTROYING THE CRIMINAL JUSTICE SYSTEM

▼ ▼ ▼ ▼ ▼

SUSAN ESTRICH

▼ ▼ ▼

▼

Harvard University Press
Cambridge, Massachusetts
London, England
1998

Library of Congress Cataloging-in-Publication Data

Estrich, Susan.
Getting away with murder : how politics is destroying
the criminal justice system / Susan Estrich.
p.   cm.
Includes bibliographical references and index.
ISBN 0-674-35411-7
1. Criminal justice, Administration of—United States.
2. Law and politics.   I. Title.
KF9223.E85   1998
345.73'05—dc21   97-41527

Designed by Gwen Frankfeldt

TO MARTY

Acknowledgments

My thanks to all those who taught me criminal law over the years, both students and teachers; the mistakes are mine.

I am especially grateful to Scott Bice, the Dean of the University of Southern California Law School, and to my colleagues and students at USC for their support, friendship, and, in the case of the students and the library staff, endless citation checking.

Thanks also to Aida Donald and Susan Wallace Boehmer at Harvard University Press, to Amanda Urban, Kathleen Sullivan, Diane Wayne, and Bert Fields. Special thanks, as always, to Marty and to Isabel and James.

Contents

Getting Away With Murder

Prologue

Beware what you wish for. After a string of high-profile acquittals in which juries have been accused of nullifying the law and letting guilty defendants get away with murder, along comes a jury that enforces the law and holds a sympathetic defendant guilty of murder. And what happens? The public is aghast, and the respected presiding judge concludes that even though the evidence is sufficient to support the verdict, it should nonetheless be reduced. "Justice" demands that Louise Woodward get away with murder.

In our society, the majority decides what the law should be, something we all recognize as a political decision. But in its application, the law is supposed to be nonpolitical: everyone is to be treated "the same," according to "the rules." The problem is that deciding who is and isn't "the same" is itself a political judgment. So is interpreting the rules. So is deciding when to ignore them.

The line between murder and manslaughter is generally the intent of the defendant: hit men are worse than drag racers. But the law also allows people to be convicted of murder if they act very recklessly, while it allows intentional and even premeditated killers to be found guilty only of manslaughter if they were provoked. It all depends on how reasonable or un-reasonable they are. But what's reasonable? The jury is bound to follow the law, except that it's free in practice to ignore it; and the judge is not to second-guess the jury, except that he has the power to nullify its decision, even if it did just what he instructed, if he decides its decision isn't just.

When I was a first-year law student at Harvard, I took the course called Legal Process with Dean Albert Sacks. The course was based on materials he'd put together nearly twenty years earlier with Henry Hart, one of the giants of legal scholarship. Legal process was, in its time, considered a brilliant response to the postwar realists' unmasking of law. The realist critique left no doubt that judges make as well as interpret law, guided by their values. In the rules of legal decision making—respect for precedent, reasoned elaboration, neutral principles—the legal process found the constraints that gave its product legitimacy as the rule of law and not simply the choices of men.

The crits—the critical legal studies advocates—thought of the legal process as a marvelous dinosaur, and the fact that the materials, twenty years later, were still bound together by staples instead of hardcovers added to their mirth. "I should be teaching the legal process," the crits' colorful and brilliant leader, Duncan Kennedy, used to say, but they wouldn't let him, and he didn't have tenure yet. In his hands, the legal process would have been a case study of deconstruction—a long semester whose point was that there wasn't a point, that everything could be manipulated, that if you pushed the so-called rules far enough, the underlying political choices would be naked. He didn't need to teach the legal process to do that, of course. You can teach any course that way.

And then what? If it's all political, then what?

Then janitors should make as much as professors. Admission to the law school should be by lottery. Law review as an elite institution should be abolished. The distinctions we drew were ultimately meaningless, or at least no more meaningful than any other. Our enterprise, our process, was delusion and denial. So said Duncan.

It infuriated me. Duncan and I had a running disagreement about it for years, one that flared with issues like affirmative action on the law review, which he favored as a way of attacking the fiction of meritocracy, and which I opposed, at least for women, as unnecessary and stigmatizing, potentially closing off one of the few avenues for women to prove, as they had to, that they were better than the men. He used to describe it as the problem of my "working-class" roots, which amused me, since my parents, first-generation Americans, prided themselves on being solidly middle class. That Duncan could say it, and I could feel it, was a measure of the distance between us.

I used to be envious of people like Duncan—well-born, educated in fancy prep schools, privy to a hundred secrets and a world of contacts way beyond mine. I went to college and law school on scholarship. My father died while I was in law school. When I graduated, I didn't have a dime, and I certainly didn't have any family connections. But I went to work for one of the top law firms in the country, for a great judge and then a great Justice, and then a great professor who has become a Justice, not to mention every Democratic presidential candidate of the 1980s, which was an eye-opening experience even when they all lost. I also became a tenured professor at Harvard Law School, and then left to take a chaired professorship at the University of Southern California Law School.

I was able to do all those things because I was smart, as measured by all the meaningless criteria—grades, law review membership, *Law Review*'s first woman president—that Duncan disparaged. However arbitrary, however contextual, the rules had opened doors for me; if they were arbitrary, at least by the time

I got there it was a form of open-door arbitrariness. If you could win at their game, they weren't allowed to deny you. In those days, the aim of antidiscrimination efforts was just to get a chance to play by the boys' rules. I didn't think of it as a working-class argument. For me, it was a feminist argument.

The feminism that descended from critical legal studies was of a more radical, separatist variety. It rightly exposed the bias inherent in neutral rules, making clear that boys' rules too often were just that—applicable only to the boys—and this exposé was itself an enormous intellectual and political achievement. But many radical feminists also rejected the possibility that *any* common rules could be fair rules, and they used the power imbalance between men and women to justify an approach that essentially says women should always win because they have always lost in the past. Similarly, critical race studies, another descendent, views law as enforcing the power of whites over blacks; academic advocacy of race-based jury nullification is squarely within this worldview. Every question is seen in gender or race terms. Race or gender always matters; it is the only thing that matters; distrust is the underlying attitude, and cynicism its expression. Better anarchy than oppression.

Or, as has been argued a million times since the O. J. Simpson verdict, whites have gotten away with murdering blacks for centuries; why is everyone so angry about a black man getting away with it every now and then?

I once had a student who learned the lessons of his first year in law school too well. By spring, when it was my turn to teach him, he thought the question of how the Supreme Court might decide a particular case to be a naive and foolish one, certainly unworthy of his attention. It's all politics, he said to me, as if that ended the discussion.

In my book, it's the beginning. There are many different ways of doing politics. My parents, faced with unfamiliar names on a ballot, would always vote for the Jew. I vote for women. This is a perfectly acceptable way to do politics in an election, particularly when you don't know who any of the commissioner candidates are. But it is not an acceptable way to do politics inside the criminal justice system.

Respect for the rule of law demands that people trust the system both to protect the innocent and to punish the guilty. A state that is too weak is as dangerous as one that is too strong. The latter invites repression; the former, anarchy, lawlessness, private justice. It is the balance that provides the grounding for a stable democracy. And vice versa.

Three-quarters of all blacks in America believe that the criminal justice system is racist and unfair. Nearly half of all whites think it's ineffective, and getting worse, particularly in dealing with issues of race.[1] The belief that the system is broken and cannot be trusted is true enough to threaten our faith not only in the rule of law but in one another.

O. J. Simpson was hardly a typical defendant, and his case was unique in many respects. But it was not as unusual as it should have been. The sense that the worst of our balkanized politics had overtaken the criminal justice system was a familiar one; the chorus that no one is responsible for anything anymore has been much repeated, before and since. If the criminal justice system was on trial, it proved guilty as charged of too-familiar crimes: abandoning the requirements of responsibility, converting juries into instruments of race politics, dividing us into our separate camps with charges of bias on all our lips, led by lawyers. The Simpson case, for all its uniqueness, captured too well the ills of the system; it is in all the ways that it is *not* unusual that the case teaches us the most.

Drawing political lines is the business of law. Was Judge Zobel "right" to let Louise Woodward get away with murder? Appeals courts can answer that because they are empowered to do so, not because those judges necessarily know better than Judge Zobel. We all can offer opinions, some of them more informed by the rules of precedent, or by how similar cases are treated, or by history or example. But in the end, we are still drawing lines on slippery slopes. Faith in the rule of law depends on our faith in one another. This book is an argument for politics as a source of faith.

Chapter 1 argues that criminal law, even in its purest and most academic incarnation, depends for its authority on the possibility of political compromise and consensus. Having a plethora of standards—what the public thinks of as "abuse excuses"—is the wrong answer to just demands for equality, but it is the answer that a mistrustful and divided society will inevitably produce. While the rule of law does not require homogeneity, it does require trust and faith in our ability to judge one another as we would ourselves. I use the familiar chestnuts of academic criminal law to illustrate how traditional tensions take on political content, leaving the common law idea of responsibility vulnerable to a lowest-common-denominator search for false equality.

Chapter 2 addresses the question not of *whether* juries should do politics but *how*, arguing that group-based jury nullification, like group-based abuse excuses, is precisely the wrong answer to the biases of the criminal justice system. There is no denying that the system is racist, albeit not in the simplistic sense that its critics often emphasize. The inevitability of racism in a system in which race and crime correlate so highly mandates attention to issues of representation and demands strict scrutiny of race-based stereotypes, precisely because they are based in fact. But to go beyond process and standards and use the power of juries to nullify the law to send a message about racism is a political disaster on all counts, sure to widen political divisions, increase crime, distort political debate, and undermine the rule of law.

Chapter 3 examines what is most easily recognized as the politics of crime: politicians who outdo one another to prove who is toughest, legislatures that pass tough-sounding but unenforceable laws, and judges who are blamed when things inevitably go wrong. The current political debate about crime distorts the allocation of power within the criminal justice system, contributes to perceptions of racism, ignores the hard questions, and deals dishonestly with the questions that are addressed. Political reactions that should be part of the solution to the loss of faith in the system instead have become part of the problem.

Chapter 4 focuses on lawyers and the intersection between professionalism and politics. The question of how far a criminal defense lawyer should go in defending a client raises in classic form some of the problems of professionalism that confront all lawyers today. Are we simply hired guns, in the business of helping our clients get away with murder, or are other values at stake that should limit and guide our actions? Should a lawyer argue that her client was framed, when she has no reason to believe that he was? Should she impeach the testimony of a witness, even though she knows the witness is telling the truth? Does she help a witness whom she doesn't believe is telling the truth prepare his testimony for trial so as to be more credible? Does she ask the jury to draw inferences, when she knows there is no basis for them? Does she try to undermine the credibility of a rape victim by invoking her sexual past and humiliating her on the stand, even if consent is not an issue? Should a lawyer play the race card, even if there is no evidence of racism? Should he attack a witness for his sexual orientation, playing to the prejudices and homophobia of a jury—or threaten to do so, in the hopes of intimidating the witness into changing his testimony or refusing to cooperate with the prosecution? Does he delay, deceive, and intimidate, in order to help his client get away with murder? Most lawyers don't, but that is not how the public sees us, or even how we view ourselves.

This book is an argument for political honesty, not political correctness. The processes of the common law need not produce results that clothe racism and sexism with the cloak of legitimacy, as its critics have rightly charged; they can also produce results that clothe commonality with the cloak of legitimacy, which a diverse society desperately needs. Cynicism is built on distrust, and uncommon law is its expression. Common law must be built on good faith.

ONE

Politics and the Reasonable Man

A white man shoots his black assailants on the subway, because he is afraid they will kill or maim him. Is it murder, manslaughter, or no crime at all? A black man shoots the racist who taunts him. Is it murder, manslaughter, or no crime at all? A mother kills a child abuser. A husband kills his unfaithful wife. A battered woman kills her husband. Two abused sons shoot an abusive father in the back.

Throw the book at them all? It won't do. Let me tell you about this father shot by his sons. He played shooting games with his kids, with real bullets. He sexually abused both sons, and then turned his attentions to their younger sister. When *his* sister reported him to social service officials, he threatened to kill her. After the shooting, his own father, the boys' grandfather, said they did the right thing. We don't really want to punish those two boys as murderers, lock them up for life without possibility of parole, do we? These are not the Menendez brothers. Lines must be drawn, not based on the race of the victim or the wealth of the defendant, but based on the law.

I teach criminal law to first-year law students. It is not criminal law as practiced in the system every day, where everyone knows that deals are being made. What I teach is the stuff of the "high church," the effort to state clearly, if only for academic and appellate purposes, the rules of criminal responsibility. If there were a place in the system that could be free from politics, this would be it. It isn't. It is political to its core.

The standard of criminal responsibility is a political compromise enforced as law. It always has been. That's its genius. The common law is a system for achieving compromise and setting common standards, for deciding who gets what, when, where, and how (the literal definition of politics) and giving legitimacy (the force of law) to those decisions.

From a distance, it doesn't look like politics at all. Under the Constitution, the criminal law must be stated clearly in advance. All states have criminal codes, most of them based on the Model Penal Code drafted in 1954 by the most respected lawyers, judges, and academics in the country as a guide for the states.[1] We have hundreds of years of case law about what the terms in these codes mean and about what satisfies their requirements and what doesn't. Judges are bound to follow the decisions of higher courts in interpreting statutes; juries are told to follow the directions of judges.

Choice is at the core of criminal liability. The person who *chooses* to kill is more blameworthy than the one who acts out of foolishness or inattention, as Justice Holmes recognized. Even a dog knows the difference between being tripped over and being stepped on. Capacity to choose sets the threshold for criminal liability. Small children are treated differently from adults. The insanity defense recognizes that a defendant must have the mental capacity to appreciate and control his conduct before he can be held criminally responsible for it.

The deliberateness of the choice is in turn measured by *mens rea*, or criminal intent. Criminal intent is divided into four basic categories: purpose (acting with a conscious object—the worst); knowledge (doing something with virtual certainty of the bad result, which is essentially the same as doing it on purpose); recklessness (knowing a risk is an unreasonable risk, and taking it anyway); and negligence (taking an unreasonable risk, whether you know it or not). Murders are graded according to the intent of the killer: The hit man, who acts on purpose, is worse than the drunk driver, who acts recklessly; the reckless driver who deliberately runs a stop sign is worse than the careless one who doesn't even see the stop sign.

Some crimes are defined in terms that require a conscious purpose: attempted murder, for instance, requires that you act with the purpose of actually killing. And being negligent is generally not a crime at all, unless it results in death; even then, mere negligence—the civil standard that would give rise to a duty to compensate the victim's family—is generally not enough to warrant criminal punishment.

Indeed, in 1962, in *Robinson v. California*, the Supreme Court came close to holding that punishing an individual in the absence of some sort of a choice violated the United States Constitution. In throwing out as cruel and unusual punishment a California statute that made it an offense to "be addicted to the use of narcotics," the Court emphasized that narcotic addiction is an illness, "which may be contracted innocently or involuntarily." The implication was that it might be unconstitutional to punish someone for something he couldn't help, couldn't control.

The four established purposes of punishment—deterrence, incapacitation, rehabilitation, and retribution—are all served by the focus on the will of the defendant. Those who do bad things on purpose are, depending on one's perspective, dangerous and deserving of being locked up (incapacitation) and/or unsocialized and in need of rehabilitation. The prospect of punishment is supposed to deter this person (specific deterrence) and others in the community (general deterrence) from making this wrong choice in the future. To punish in the absence of choice, it is argued by many, cannot deter: how can you deter someone from doing something he didn't choose to do? And as for retribution, aren't we all angrier at the person who intentionally runs down a child than at the person who does it by accident?

To punish in the absence of choice, scholars and judges have argued, is morally unjust: punishment requires fault, and fault requires the ability to do otherwise. If a person was doing the best he could, even if he failed to meet society's standards, the prospect of punishment would not deter him, and its imposition would be unfair. The House of Lords, England's highest court, adopted a variant of this position in the controversial 1976 case of *Regina v. Morgan,* where the Justices concluded that three drunken sailors could not be convicted of rape if they believed, honestly but unreasonably, that the woman they were raping was screaming and fighting because it made sex more exciting for her, as their buddy—the husband of the victim—had allegedly told them.

Requiring choice works just fine, except when it doesn't—when, as in *Morgan,* the result of requiring choice seems to violate common sense. Even the most enthusiastic proponents of choice, even those who would excuse an individual who makes an unreasonable mistake, have their limits. It may be impossible to deter someone who is out of control, but no one wants to license a hothead to kill—even if he is congenitally short-tempered. Do we really care that he wasn't "choosing" fully? In their retrial, the *Morgan* defendants were again convicted; the jury either didn't believe them, or didn't care.

The law in many jurisdictions distinguishes between first- and second-degree murder based on premeditation and deliberation—a measure of the intensity of the choice. But taken literally in every case, such a distinction produces unjustifiable results. The man who kills his spouse after years of mental and physical abuse of himself and their children ends up guilty of a more serious crime (premeditated murder) than the murderer who stabs his girlfriend's 10-year-old daughter 60 times in a sudden act of senseless rage. The resolution adopted by most jurisdictions is to require premeditation but to hold that it can be done in a matter of seconds. So much for measuring the intensity of choice.

Of course, it also doesn't work to punish everyone who produces a bad result, regardless of their state of mind. That may be acceptable at least in some circumstances in tort law, where what is involved is monetary compensation for the injured party; but even in tort law, strict liability remains controversial. Certainly it would be unjust, as well as a huge waste of resources, to impose strict liability broadly in the criminal law, to deprive people of life and liberty for every mistake, to turn every car accident into an assault, much less a murder. It would be hard to find anyone, even in politics, who wanted to hold everyone criminally accountable for the harms they cause, to tolerate no excuses at all, not even partial ones. There are differences among those who produce the same result, even if all the people they kill are equally dead.

So how do we decide? What is the law? The law is what the "reasonable person" would do—in the old days, the "reasonable man." His actions and reactions provide the guide to when an intentional killing is murder and when it isn't, when conduct is criminally reckless and when it isn't, when self-defense is legitimate and when it isn't, when provocation is sufficient and when it isn't.

Consider the problem of mistaken self-defense. You kill someone because you honestly believe that if you don't, he really will shoot that gun and kill you. You turn out to be wrong. He wasn't armed. The gun wasn't loaded. The intruder was just a neighborhood kid. Are you guilty of murder? Manslaughter? No crime at all?

The answer, of course, is that it depends. "Detached reflection is not required in the presence of an uplifted knife," as Justice Oliver Wendell Holmes put it.[2] Or a gun. Were you mistaken because you were attacked in the dark, or because you are physically blind, or because you were too drunk to see straight? Did you believe the kid was going to kill you because he reached into his pocket and uttered threatening words, or because you flashed back to your experiences in Vietnam, or because he was black?

Drawing lines turns out to be a far messier process than choosing among a hierarchy of intents. All lives have equal value in the eyes of the law—except that, of course, they don't. No one should take the law into their own hands, but only a law student afraid of being stuck on a slippery slope would be reluctant to distinguish between the child abuser who kills an innocent child and the angry parent who kills the child abuser. Both kill on purpose; killing is still wrong; but killing for a reason all of us can relate to is not quite so wrong as killing a child.

Self-defense justifies murder, provided the reasonable man would have also responded with deadly force. Provocation is a partial excuse, provided that the defendant's loss of control was reasonable. Unintentional wrongdoing or negligence will not be punished, unless the risk you took was unreasonable. The reasonable man allows society to set standards for itself, as it should.

But who is this reasonable man? Who does he look like? How much does he look like the defendant? The more the reasonable man resembles the defendant, the more reasonable the defendant's actions will appear to be.

A classic and much-cited statement of self-defense law can be found in the 1849 New York case of *Shorter v. People*. The defendant in *Shorter* was a young black man, fifteen at the time of the killing, who was aroused by a racial slur and attacked his victim, initially with his fists and later with a knife. The trial judge, over defense counsel's objection, had instructed the jury that an actual danger to the defendant was required in order to allow his use of self-defense; the defense lawyer had requested an instruction that a reasonable fear was enough. The appeals court reversed; the trial judge was clearly wrong; a requirement of actual danger "would lay too heavy a burden upon poor humanity."

But the court went on to make clear that it was not enough that the defendant believed himself to be in danger; the jury must also find reasonable grounds for that belief. While some scholars have argued that *Shorter* was wrongly decided—a misreading of English law, it is argued, leading to the imposition of unjust punishment upon those who cannot or did not choose to murder—its language has become legal boilerplate. Self-defense requires not only that the defendant think he or another was in imminent danger but also that his belief be reasonable.

The law of provocation works much the same way. Provocation is what distinguishes intentional killings that are murder from those treated as the much less serious crime of manslaughter. The doctrine of provocation emerged in sixteenth-century England as a means to spare those who killed in sudden, and sometimes drunken, quarrels, or for breaches of honor, from the automatic penalty of death that followed a conviction of murder. In 1628 Coke defined manslaughter as being "upon a sudden occasion; and therefore is called a chance-medley." In a killing by chance-medley, according to Coke, "all that followed was but a continuance of the first sudden occasion, and the heat of blood kindled by ire was never cooled, till blow was given." By the eighteenth century, chance-medley had disappeared as its own category, incorporated into a more general doctrine that partially excused killings committed in the heat of passion.

In order to reduce an intentional killing from murder to voluntary manslaughter, though, it's not enough that the defendant lost control. The loss of control must be reasonable; there must be a "reasonable explanation or excuse" for it.[3] Of course, reasonable people don't kill when provoked; they don't lose control and kill in an angry rage; that's why such conduct is prohibited by law. The only time it is reasonable to kill is in self-defense. In this context, reasonableness is less a normative standard than an empathic one. A woman tells a man she no longer wants to date him. In a rage, he kills her. Should he be treated the same, as a matter of law, as the parent who kills the child abuser? Certainly not.

In *Hill v. State* (1918), a murder conviction was reversed after a judge instructed the jury that the defendant could not have killed in self-defense since his attacker was threatening him only with his fists. "It is doubtless true that one may not, ordinarily, repel the attack of an unarmed man by killing him. There may be many cases in which the disparity between the combatants is so overwhelming that the one of superior power may inflict great bodily harm." The rule was soon widely accepted that the reasonable person was the same size and strength of the defendant.

Physical disabilities came next. Bad health, bad eyesight, a bandage on the hand, and missing fingers were all accepted by American courts as characteristics of the defendant which could be shared with the reasonable man, and which qualified the objectivity of the standard.

The reasonable person also was given the defendant's knowledge of his victim's history of violence. If the defendant knew that his victim was usually armed, or had a reputation for violence, this would be admissible; indeed, in some jurisdictions, it would be admissible even if the defendant didn't know about it.

But where do you draw the line? In the famous English case of *Bedder v. Director of Public Prosecutions* (1954), a young man killed a prostitute who taunted him for his impotence and kicked him "in the privates." He was convicted of murder after the trial judge instructed the jury that it should apply the standard of "the reasonable person, the ordinary person" in evaluating the defendant's claim of provocation, and that his sexual impotence did not entitle him "to rely on provocation which would not have led an ordinary person to have acted" as he did. The House of Lords affirmed the conviction, refusing to recognize in sexual impotence the sort of physical disability that would justify an adjustment to the reasonable-man standard.

In a later case in which a fifteen-year-old killed the man who sexually assaulted and laughed at him, the court explicitly declined to follow *Bedder*, ruling that the jury should be allowed to "take into consideration all those factors which in their opinion would affect the gravity of taunts or insults when applied to the person to whom they are addressed."

"Better or worse?" I ask my students, like the doctor trying on different lenses to diagnose nearsightedness. Except that we are comparing killers, not the clarity of images. We ask questions; out of the answers come patterns; out of the patterns, rules. It feels like an objective process, not like choosing your candidate. Hands fly. People "know" the answer. Sometimes we all agree, and it doesn't feel like politics at all—more like Sunday school. There can still be right and wrong on a slippery slope. But we don't spend much time on easy cases; you teach common law by teaching hard cases.

Like the case of Mrs. Burke, the long-suffering (and maybe abused) isolated farm wife in the classic novella and film *Jury of*

Her Peers, who strangles her sleeping husband after he strangles her beloved bird.[4] The sheriff's wife and a woman neighbor find the dead bird among her sewing things, while the men are off searching for some evidence of a motive that will tie her to the killing. The women hide the evidence. A jury of her peers, or obstruction of justice? Is she a murderer? Half the class say yes: premeditated and deliberate. Manslaughter? Almost as many hands. Excused as self-defense? Always a few, sometimes more. What is reasonable? What does the reasonable person/woman do?

In the old days, by the third week of class, my students would start glaring, convinced that I somehow knew the answer and was just unwilling to tell them, that once I tired of toying with them, once I'd played the Kingsfield/*Paper Chase* routine through, I would say the magic words—or the guy next to them would figure it out. These days, I tell them the first day. I don't have an answer. There's just the reasonable man.

My students think of the reasonable man as a cop-out, and an untidy one at that. I think of him as a bit of genius, both inevitable and necessary. The reasonable man is the civic standard of responsibility, what we demand and expect of one another. We insist on a defendant's having a choice only to a point; beyond that point, we impose accountability. Where it is reasonable to set that point is a political question; the common law of the reasonable man gives form to an inherently political exercise. Lines do emerge, even if rules can be broken.

The common law rules that have emerged over the last two centuries have much to commend them. They incorporate great respect for the value of human life, along with expectations of restraint. Words alone are not enough to provoke. Outside of the home, one is required to retreat, if it can be done safely, before using deadly force. The threat of harm, if it is to justify deadly force in self-defense, must be imminent. If you're claiming provocation, there can be no cooling off period between the provocation and the use of force; if you have time to cool off, you're expected to do so.

But the rules, and the patterns of their application, also incorporate the bias of those who framed them. They are the product of the process that produced them, a process almost exclusively conducted by white men. Shorter received no special consideration because he was the black victim of racist taunts, any more than did Bedder, the impotent victim of the prostitute's taunts. The reasonable man is not black and not impotent. If the 1950s were a time of greater clarity in the law, it is not because politics was missing but because the homogeneity of the system made consensus look and feel like something other than a political decision. The areas of disagreement were narrower; the areas of commonality were broader; the decision makers, most of them anyway, saw the world through the same set of experiences.

The first recognized exception to the rule that a battery—a touching—was required to constitute adequate provocation was marital infidelity. Adultery was considered an interference with property, while an unfaithful fiancée did not even partially excuse a killing. Doctrinally, the wife's unfaithfulness reduced the crime from murder to manslaughter; in practice, it usually excused it entirely. Indeed, four states explicitly recognized "the honor defense," and most others did in practice. In 1868 a defense attorney who was representing a husband who had killed his wife's lover with an axe was able to argue that "no jury had ever convicted a husband of any offense, under such a state of facts, either in England or in this country."

In many places the jealous-husband defense continues to be the most routine way of getting away with murder. If O. J. Simpson hadn't been famous, and if his victims had been the same race as he is, then he might well have been able to portray himself as the classic jealous husband, happening upon his wife with another man, a good guy who lost it for a moment and who should be charged only with manslaughter. Of course, he and his wife were divorced, but their relationship was hardly over, and she would have been portrayed as no angel. One of Robert Shapiro's former clients won his fifteen minutes of fame early in the case by recounting the great deal Shapiro had negotiated on his behalf in similar circumstances. He killed his wife, and he was out in five.

What's striking is that O. J. Simpson could not be offered that deal because, in 1996, a manslaughter bargain would have been politically untenable. The problem is that this politically untenable result has continued to be rather routine in the system when people who are not famous are involved, and it has added ammunition to the assault on the reasonable man among critical legal theorists.

Compare the treatment of Kenneth Peacock, a Maryland man whose sentencing in the same summer of 1994 attracted attention only because of its parallels to the Simpson case. The noncelebrity defendant was a long-distance truck driver who drank heavily, as did his wife. The two had been married six years, with frequent separations, when he returned unexpectedly one night at midnight and found her in bed with another man. He forced the other man to leave, and then he and his wife began arguing, and drinking. Some hours later, he shot and killed his wife; in a call to the 911 operator after 4 A.M., he said he killed his wife "because she was sleeping around on him." Mr. Peacock did not have a record of criminal convictions although, it emerged later, he had threatened his wife in the past because of her infidelity, and on one occasion he had beaten her so badly that she took refuge in a guarded hotel room. Two of his brothers are Baltimore police officers. The victim was an eighth-grade dropout, married four times.

The prosecutor's office agreed not to charge Peacock with murder (even though he had time to cool down) in exchange for his plea of guilty to the crime of manslaughter (*State v. Peacock*). In Maryland, the maximum sentence for voluntary manslaughter is ten years. In Peacock's case, the prosecution recommended a sentence of three to eight years—which means that Mr. Peacock, with good behavior, would only have to serve two. The sentencing judge decided even that was too harsh, substituting an eighteen-month sentence, with work release, so he could keep his job.

"I cannot think of a circumstance whereby personal rage is more uncontrollable . . . than this for someone who is happily married. I shudder to think what I would do . . . I seriously wonder how many married men, married five years or four years, would have the strength to walk away . . . without inflicting some corporal punishment," said Judge Robert E. Cahill Sr. of the Baltimore County Circuit Court. A few weeks later, a woman was given a longer sentence in the same circuit court for killing her abusive husband. The judge in that case apparently did not relate so easily to her plight.

The vulnerability of the common law to political attack is not limited to its comparative treatment of angry husbands and abused wives. The common law also accepts, indeed celebrates, a certain brand of machismo whose anthem is "Make my day." Its roots in chance-medley are still apparent, and cases of this sort tend to enjoy a profile that makes them count for more in our understanding and acceptance of the laws than their actual numbers might merit.

The most famous such case involved Bernhard Goetz, who shot four young black men on a New York City subway on December 22, 1984. Goetz was a hero in New York, even though his own version of events failed the traditional requirements of self-defense: he continued shooting after the danger to him, even if he had been "reasonable" about that, had disappeared. The first grand jury refused to indict him, and the jury that ultimately heard the criminal case refused to convict him of anything more than a weapons offense *(People v. Goetz)*. Ten years later, a second jury, this one composed only of minorities, imposed damages of $43 million on a bankrupt Goetz in a civil suit brought by the most seriously injured victim.

The question of who the reasonable man is, and what he does on the subway, was the central legal issue in Goetz's criminal trial. After Goetz was finally indicted for attempted murder, his attorneys convinced first the trial court and then the appellate court to throw out the indictment on the ground that the prosecutor had improperly instructed the grand jury to apply an "objective" standard to the self-defense determination. Goetz, they managed to argue successfully, should be judged based on the way he saw things, not the way a reasonable man who didn't share all his traits would. The New York Court of Appeals finally reversed. One hundred years after *Shorter,* the same court reaffirmed its rejection of a subjective test, emphasizing that New York had not adopted the approach urged by the drafters of the Model Penal Code that would allow even unreasonable mistakes of fact to serve as a partial excuse for murder if the individual honestly believed deadly force was necessary. In New York, the court held, the reasonable person is the only guide to justifiable self-defense.

But who is this reasonable man? How much like Goetz is he? A determination of reasonableness, the court emphasized, must be based on the "circumstances" facing a defendant or his "situation." "Such terms encompass more than the physical movement of the potential assailant . . . These terms include any relevant knowledge the defendant had about that person. They also necessarily bring in the physical attributes of the persons involved, including the defendant. Furthermore, the defendant's circumstances encompass any prior experiences he had which could provide a reasonable basis for a belief that another person's intentions were to injure or rob him or that the use of deadly force was necessary under the circumstances." During the trial, Goetz's lawyer succeeded at drawing a vivid picture of the scariness of the subways.

Every year, it seems, there is another Goetz case—another case that commands public attention, in which a man, usually white, is celebrated for shooting and killing thugs, often minorities. In Los Angeles, 1995's Goetz was William Masters, who confronted two graffiti taggers in his neighborhood, started writing down their license number, and then shot and killed one of them, claiming self-defense. The taggers were Hispanics; Masters was white. After a much publicized review, the District Attorney's office decided to charge him with only a weapons violation. Many in the Hispanic community claimed that Masters had gotten away with murder, particularly after he was quoted as describing his victims as "wetbacks." Many others believed that he should not have been charged with any crime, and celebrated him as a hero.

If you excuse Goetz and Masters because you can identify with them, because you're afraid on the subway, because you hate taggers, then why shouldn't lawyers for battered wives and abused sons be able to prove that their clients are no worse, and that the men they kill are no better than the thugs or the taggers—household rather than street criminals? If Goetz's life experiences are valid, why not Shorter's or Bedder's? The modern political attack on the criminal law is an attack on the reasonable man as being racist and sexist, Western and white. If white men get away with murder, why not everyone?

▼   ▼   ▼

In many respects, *State v. Wanrow* in 1979 marks the starting point of this political assault on the reasonable man. It is the first of the major women's self-defense cases, most of which involved battered women. But Avena Wanrow didn't kill her husband. She killed William Wesler, a man she strongly suspected of child abuse. Her son said the man had tried to drag him off his bicycle; her friend, Ms. Hopper, believed he was the man who had sexually abused her seven-year-old daughter, giving her a venereal disease; her landlord recognized him, when he came to deny the allegations, and told her that he had tried to seduce a boy who had previously lived there and had been confined in a mental institution in the past.

Ms. Hopper called the police and asked that they arrest the man, but was told that nothing could be done until Monday. The two women decided to spend the night together, with their children, and Wanrow arrived with a pistol in her handbag. Wanrow's sister and brother-in-law joined them there for the night at the request of the two women. Apparently without the defendant's knowledge, her brother-in-law went over to the man's house at 5 A.M., armed with a baseball bat, and accused him of molesting the children. He denied it, and suggested they go over to the Hopper home to straighten things out.

Now things get murkier. Wesler, a large man, entered the house. Wanrow's brother-in-law remained outside. Wesler was apparently intoxicated. There was a good deal of shouting. Mrs. Wanrow, who stood 5'4" and was using a crutch for a broken leg, testified that she went to the door to call her brother-in-law; when she turned around, she found Wesler standing right behind her, was gravely startled, and shot him.

Did she kill him because she was afraid and believed she needed to defend herself and the children, or because she was angry and took the law into her own hands? Did she lose control and kill in a sudden rage, or was it an intentional and deliberate act of vengeance against a man who had never been convicted of anything? The jury convicted her of second-degree murder, rejecting her claims of self-defense and provocation.

On appeal, Mrs. Wanrow's attorneys claimed that the judge and jury had erred in failing to take into account her cultural background—she is a Native American—and in judging her according to the standard of a "reasonable man." The trial court, in instructing the jury, had told them that it was appropriate to take into account the "relative size and strength" of the persons involved, but the rest of the instructions were phrased in masculine terms. The trial court did not ask the jury to compare Mrs. Wanrow to a reasonable *man;* but it did speak of someone trying to kill "him" or inflict upon "him" great bodily harm. The impression created, according to the Supreme Court of Washington, was that "the objective standard to be applied is that applicable to an altercation between two men."

Quoting U.S. Supreme Court decisions on sex discrimination rarely invoked in criminal cases, the court held that "the respondent was entitled to have the jury consider her actions in the light of her own perceptions of the situation, including those perceptions which were the product of 'our nation's long and unfortunate history of sex discrimination.' Until such time as the effects of that history are eradicated, care must be taken to assure that our self-defense instructions afford women the right to have their conduct judged in light of the individual physical handicaps which are the product of sex discrimination." The instructions of the trial court "misstates our law in creating an objective standard of 'reasonableness.' It then compounds that error by utilizing language suggesting that the respondent's conduct must be measured against that of a reasonable male individual finding himself in the same circumstances."

Are women entitled to their own instructions on self-defense because they are women? Should the standard of responsibility be changed when they are the victims of discrimination?

Professor Elizabeth Schneider, who served as Wanrow's attorney on appeal, explains the line of women's self-defense cases that begins with *Wanrow* as a response to the dominance of male norms in the law. Battered women's defenses, Professor Schneider argues, were intended to overcome the sex bias in the law of self-defense and to equalize the treatment of women in the courts.[5]

In 1979 Lenore Walker published a book describing the cycles of violence often involved in battering relationships, and the syndrome that keeps women in such relationships. According to Dr. Walker, there are three stages in battering cycles: the tension-building stage, which tends to involve minor battering and verbal abuse by the man, while the woman tries to placate him; the acute battering incident, which may be triggered by external events in the life of the man or by the reaction of the woman; and contrition, the stage in which the man is loving and begs for forgiveness. Battered women tend to remain in these relationships both because of the cyclical nature of the abuse and because of the passivity, low self-esteem, sense of responsibility, and ultimately paralysis which, Dr. Walker and others have argued, are typical manifestations of the syndrome.[6]

For much of the 1980s the admissibility of expert testimony about battered women's syndrome (often by Dr. Walker herself) has been debated in American courts and legislatures. Whether Walker's research is scientifically valid has been questioned; it has been the subject of significant critical review. Even so, in most states, feminist attorneys and advocates have successfully persuaded judges and legislatures to admit the testimony of such experts.

There is more than a little irony to this particular "feminist triumph," and it has left many feminists, including Professor Schneider herself, somewhat discomfited. For one thing, there is the seeming inconsistency of using a syndrome rooted in learned passivity to justify the ultimate act of aggression—murder. Whatever may be true of battered women in general is not necessarily true of the minority of them who kill. Worse, here you have feminists arguing to incorporate into the law the very sort of stereotypes of women as weak, passive, lovelorn, and ultimately not responsible that it has taken decades to get rid of in the culture.

The initial reason accepted for the evidence of battered women's syndrome was that it helped stop the chain of argument that began from the premise that if things were as bad as she said, she would have left, and concluded that the woman must therefore be lying. Those unfamiliar with battering relationships may find it hard to believe what women endure, and with what silence, from men who couldn't be nicer to others. In that sense, the expert adds to credibility, and if the judge concludes that the science is decent and the jury could use help, it gets admitted.

The controversy about battered women's syndrome is not really about whether it should be permitted to bolster credibility. It is about whether it should change the standard of responsibility against which the woman is measured. Is the reasonable woman a battered woman? Advocates, Dr. Walker included, have argued that battered women should not be held to the standards of other, reasonable people; that imminence should be defined from the battered women's cycle to include the risk posed by a sleeping man; that self-defense should even allow a battered woman to hire a hit man to kill her husband if she didn't know how to do it herself and honestly believed there was no other way out of danger.

The efforts to use syndrome defenses to individualize the standard of responsibility parallel the efforts of the 1950s and 1960s to expand the insanity defense to accomplish the same result. It is ironic because one of the toughest critics of abuse excuses and the lawyers who use them, Alan Dershowitz, as well as his mentor, D.C. Circuit Chief Judge David Bazelon, were among the leaders of that earlier effort.

The traditional legal test of insanity is found in the famous *M'Naughten Case,* an 1843 decision of the House of Lords whose fact pattern is eerily reminiscent of John Hinckley's attempted assassination of President Reagan and his near-murder of Reagan's press secretary, James Brady. M'Naughten killed Edward Drummond, the secretary to then–Prime Minister Sir Robert Peel, mistaking him for Peel. His defense was that he was being persecuted and suffered from delusions. He had money, which allowed him to hire four barristers and nine medical experts. He was found by the jury to be not guilty by reason of insanity.

An uproar ensued, with the press warning that madmen could now kill freely; even Queen Victoria, herself the object of assassination attempts, expressed concern. The judges were "invited" to the House of Lords to explain their decision, and the M'Naughten rule emerged in answer to the questions. "To establish a defense of insanity, it must be clearly proved that, at the time of the committing of the act, the party accused was laboring under such a defect of reason, from disease of mind, as not to know the nature and quality of the act he was doing, or if he did know it, he did not know that it was wrong."

The test has long been criticized as being too strict in its requirement of a total lack of knowledge. Its companion test, the irresistible impulse test, was similarly criticized for requiring a total lack of control. Advocates of an expanded insanity defense argued that no one should be punished if their conduct was "the product of a mental disease or defect." Psychiatrists and their expert knowledge would guide the jury in understanding the reasons for a person's action before determining

28

▼

his guilt. We would take a tour inside his head, aided by modern science, instead of enforcing the traditional legal straitjacket.

The big victory came in 1954. As Chief Judge David Bazelon put it in his famous decision in *Durham v. United States,* "The science of psychiatry now recognizes that a man is an integrated personality and that reason, which is only one element in that personality, is not the sole determinant of his conduct." What became known as the Durham rule replaced the M'Naughten rule with an invitation to psychiatrists to share the full range of their knowledge with juries, since the defendant was not criminally responsible if his unlawful conduct could be shown to be the "product" of a "mental disease or defect."

The Durham rule didn't work. It transferred decision making from judges and juries to psychiatrists, leaving the legal system dependent on this profession in embarrassing ways. The most notorious example of this, the "weekend flip-flop," occurred when psychiatrists at Saint Elizabeths hospital in Washington, D.C., the major public mental hospital in the nation's capital, changed their minds about whether a sociopathic personality disorder should be considered a "mental disease or defect." A defendant whose trial extended over the weekend was discovered to suffer a disease or defect on Monday that he didn't have on Friday. Another defendant convicted a month earlier of murder under the old definition managed to win a new trial in light of the change. The problem extended as well to the question of what counted as a "product," and who should decide it, and whether the logic of the insanity defense should apply as well to acts which are the "product" of such conditions as poverty and "rotten social background."

While Judge Bazelon, Alan Dershowitz, and their colleagues struggled mightily to solve these problems—holding, for example, that disease or defect was a jury determination, not a psychiatric one, and limiting the ability of psychiatrists to testify as to their opinion on the "product" question—the Durham rule was ultimately replaced in the federal courts by a rule of "substantial capacity," a modification of the M'Naughten rule. The new rule, based on the Model Penal Code, requires (as opposed to M'Naughten's absolutist standard) that the defendant lack "substantial capacity" either to appreciate the wrongfulness or criminality of his conduct or to conform his conduct to the rule of law.

But what is most striking about the Durham rule, particularly in light of all the criticism, is how little difference it made, at least with juries. In the District of Columbia, insanity acquittals increased somewhat in the year *Durham* was decided, but never above 5 percent, and then dropped sharply even before the rule was abandoned. In mock studies that have been conducted by researchers, the instructions given to the jury—whether following *M'Naughten, Durham,* or the "substantial capacity" test—have been found to produce almost no differences in the conviction rates. The threshold of criminal responsibility is not a scientific standard but a political statement, itself a compromise between choice and accountability that the society, represented by a jury, makes, not the psychiatrists.

As it should. After John Hinckley was acquitted under the Model Penal Code rule, Congress and many states moved to tighten it further, and a few have even moved to eliminate the insanity defense altogether, replacing it with a verdict of "guilty but insane." The number of states recognizing diminished capacity as a defense has dwindled. The clear trend is to hold people responsible for their behavior, whatever their mental state.

Why doesn't that same answer apply to the battered wife who kills her sleeping husband, even if her response is a product of battered woman's syndrome? If it is just to punish the person suffering from mental illness when he violates the norms of society, why isn't it just to punish the person suffering from battered women's syndrome?

The reason that the same answer doesn't apply is, once again, politics. John Hinckley was a rich white male. The debate about the insanity defense was about standards of responsibility, not politics. Dr. Walker and Professor Schneider, by turning what might otherwise be seen as "disease or defect" into a gender-based syndrome, have succeeded in converting an individualized assault into a group attack, changing it from an argument about choice to one about politics. The charge is not that the system is unfair to the individual whose capacity to choose was impaired—a claim we're accustomed to rejecting when we want to—but that it discriminates against women as a group. If Peacock can kill his wife and get away with murder, why should women go to prison for killing abusive husbands? If Bernhard Goetz gets to keep shooting a black kid in the back, even if he's not sure whether the kid was ever dangerous, how can it be fair to stop a woman from shooting the white man in the back whom she knows is a thug? The battered-women's-syndrome defense is not about choice. It's about discrimination.

The women's self-defense cases are an attack on the political processes of the criminal law for excluding the voices of women, and on the results it produces for discriminating against women. "Majority rules" is no answer when the real majority is denied full participation and when the offense charged is invidious discrimination. Whites could not decide as a group to punish blacks more severely than whites, even if whites are in the majority. They certainly could not do it after excluding blacks from participating in the decision-making process. So, too, men cannot decide to punish women more severely than men.

The feminist attack invites imitation. Turn a defect into a syndrome and you have a new group of victims who can claim to have been excluded, and a result that can be attacked as discriminatory. Alan Dershowitz lists dozens of such excuses in his book on "abuse excuses."[7] My own top ten are listed in the Appendix. Creative lawyers continually add to the list. Many of the efforts misfire, but there are enough successes to contribute powerfully to the sense that everyone who can afford an expensive lawyer can avoid being held responsible for his or her behavior.

If it violates rules of equality to discriminate on the basis of gender, what about on the basis of culture and ethnic identity? The cultural assault on the standards of responsibility has taken essentially the same form as the gender assault: a demand for expert testimony; an effort to reconfigure the identity of the reasonable man; a fall-back defense of insanity, based on the same expert testimony. Its proponents argue that it is unfair that the partial excuse of provocation is only available to the dominant culture.

Consider the 1987 case of the Chinese man who bludgeoned his wife to death after she confessed to adultery. At defense counsel's request, a professor of anthropology was permitted to testify about the "enormous stain" in Chinese culture of a wife's adultery, a stain which constitutes "a reflection on his ancestors and his progeny." The judge in *People v. Chen* was apparently moved; he found the defendant guilty only of second-degree manslaughter and sentenced him to five years' probation—even less time than Kenneth Peacock had to serve.

Or consider the 1986 incident in which a Laotian refugee residing in New York stabbed his wife in a jealous rage after she got a phone call from a former boyfriend. In *People v. Aphaylath* (1986), the trial court excluded the offer of expert testimony about Laotian culture and refugee problems, holding that the jury didn't need expert evidence on the subject of jealousy. The New York Court of Appeals reversed, holding the exclusion of the expert's testimony to be an error, and a plea bargain was agreed to.

Or consider the well-known 1985 case of Fumiko Kimura, the woman who walked with her two children into the ocean in Santa Monica, enacting the ancient Japanese ritual of self-sacrifice in shame at her husband's adultery. The children died; the mother, dragged out of the ocean, survived and faced charges of murder. Relying on a cultural defense, she was allowed to plead guilty to manslaughter, with her punishment set at one year in the county jail, which she had already served, plus five years' probation with psychiatric counseling *(People v. Kimura)*.

What is so revealing about most of the syndrome/culture/abuse cases is the way they combine arguments of reasonableness with arguments of insanity. The defendant claims that either the reasonable person should be reconfigured sufficiently in the defendant's image to make the defendant's actions reasonable, or else the defendant was temporarily insane. Those are the two choices. They collapse the standards of responsibility and irresponsibility, converting the external standard of reasonableness into an internal one that might also qualify as insane. When looked at subjectively enough, behaviors that otherwise would plainly be seen as nuts are now seen as reasonable.

The logical extreme of the argument for abuse excuses, sympathy defenses, and other forms of group-based entitlement is that only hit men are murderers. Everyone else, judged by the standards of his self-defined cultural or abuse group, is doing no worse than someone just like him would do, and this, it is argued, is no worse than what white men have let one another get away with, at least as seen from an outsider's perspective, for a very long time. The effort to define responsibility reduces to a search for the lowest common denominator, a downward spiral propelled by the sense of everyone else that the standard that the common law judges thought to be a strict one seems anything but, from an outside perspective. You killed your wife because she cheated? I think abusive husbands are far worse, at least according to my eye chart.

The morning after the second Menendez trial, a time of optimism for the rule of law if not the rules of lawyering, the first question I was asked in a radio interview was whether the Menendez *sisters* would have been convicted. If they'd been young women claiming that their father had abused them throughout their girlhood, my questioner suggested, they would have walked. White men are the latest victims, some say, because they are the only ones who can't get away with murder anymore. Even O. J. Simpson can't cut a deal because the feminists would scream. Abuse of boys doesn't count for as much as abuse of girls. This is what it looks like when victimization comes full circle.

The most obvious answer is to say no to everybody: to the angry husband and the abused wife and the abused children, to the Laotians, Japanese, and Chinese, as well as the angry Americans. No special rules. Only one victim. Only try defendants. But what do you say to the Dutton brothers? In the summer of 1993, Herman and Druie Dutton, then 15 and 12 respectively, killed their father as he was sleeping on the sofa. One brother held the hunting rifle, while the other pulled the trigger. Their defense was that they were hoping to save their sister from being abused, as they had been.

The father, Lonnie Dutton, a bad-tempered, gun-loving drinker, abused his wife and tortured his children from the time they were born. According to Mr. Dutton's sister, he would thump the infants on their heads; neighbors heard the four children screaming and crying at all times of the day and night. His former wife, who left him and then lost custody of the children in a court fight, says she wished she'd killed him herself years before; Dutton used to shoot at her feet while she cooked.

According to relatives, he would also force his son to stand against their trailer while he shot a ring of bullets around his head. Both a neighbor and Dutton's sister telephoned social service officials, but the children were afraid to say anything to the authorities against their father, who threatened to kill the relatives he suspected of telephoning. When his own father objected to the way he was treating his children, Lonnie shot him and stabbed him twice, according to the father, who said his grandchildren had done the right thing in killing their father, his son. So did everyone else in the small, poor town, which formed a support group for the boys, tied ribbons, donated clothes. Every one of the father's relatives, every neighbor, took the sons' side. Six people could not be found to serve as pallbearers at Lonnie Dutton's funeral.[8]

The people of that town didn't need a psychiatric social worker or a cultural anthropologist to tell them the right thing to do in the Dutton situation. It didn't matter very much what race or religion they were, whether they were men or women, old or young. It was the common sense of the entire community that these children deserved sympathy and not punishment.

Compare the Menendez brothers. I was never convinced they were physically abused, but a number of jurors were. For the sake of argument, let's assume it. Self-defense? Not a chance. They were older, they had options, they could escape, and Dutton was a much worse man than Jose Menendez. After a second, well-run trial *(People v. Menendez)*, the Menendez brothers were convicted of murder. In the Dutton case, prosecutors reached an agreement that the brothers would plead no contest to juvenile manslaughter charges, and the case would be put off three years and then dismissed if the boys broke no other law.

It's easy in the eye-chart way. Better or worse? It's not even close. The challenge is to articulate a rule that lets the Dutton brothers off without inviting the Menendez brothers along for the ride and declaring a field day for excuses and syndromes.

The answer is obvious. If we didn't have it, we'd have to invent it. Reasonableness. The reasonable person. Not the lowest common denominator, which allows everyone to get away with murder, and not the 1950s white-male standard either, but the product of an inclusive process that seeks to define and enforce common ground. The criminal justice system deserved to be attacked for excluding the voices of women and minorities. Its version of reasonableness did reflect the will of a particular majority. But white men only look alike from the outside. They don't always agree on everything, either. Why, after all, should a man be able to kill his wife for disloyalty but not his fiancée? One is reasonable and one isn't. Why?

The statutes don't say that, and never did; they simply say that an intended killing, if provoked, is manslaughter. Logic doesn't compel it. True, marriage is a tighter bond, but why isn't engagement enough? It smells like a compromise between those who would probably punish everybody and those who would punish nobody. If you trace it down, you find it's a product of judicial opinion, academic dissection, and jury realities which then becomes part of the common law. The answer to the question "Why *this* line?" is "Because that is the law." It is a legitimate political decision, and its enforcement is the rule of law.

Can we find a single standard of reasonableness to apply to everybody? Of course not. What about the blind person? What about the kids who really are abused? Does everybody then get their own standard: one for men, one for women, one for the battered, one for the impotent? Absurd. Reasonableness then becomes a standard of unreasonableness. Lines have to be drawn. Reasonableness is the process for doing that. It is an invitation to decide. Its genius is its endless adaptability. Dueling used to be reasonable. Now it isn't.

Can reasonableness still adapt? Can we imagine a process, an inclusive and representative process, in which Americans of diverse backgrounds and beliefs could come together and decide that some battered wives are acting reasonably and some others aren't; that the Duttons should not be punished but the Menendez brothers should? Could juries become places where we find common ground and enforce it, not head to our separate camps?

Some of the common law rules might need some minor adjustments. Does the "imminence" requirement in self-defense assume that people have the capacity to protect themselves if they are not in the middle of the fight? Is that assumption more true of men than of women, of adults than kids? Maybe. But you can interpret imminence as a variant of the retreat requirement: Was there a way out, or wasn't there? Was her failure to see it, if it was there, reasonable? That's the beauty of the common law. That's the easy part.

At its essence, the balkanization of criminal responsibility raises a question about our trust in one another that extends beyond the jury room. It's not that "we" can't draw lines. It's whether "we" trust others to draw them. Do we trust others to judge as we would ourselves—to draw lines that apply to others as we would apply them to ourselves? Can a diverse society live by a common law? Can we live together any other way?

It is argued by some that any single standard is a male standard, a white standard, an unfair one, that any process, no matter how inclusive, will favor men. The mere suggestion that lines might be drawn among battered women draws wrath no matter how inclusive the system is.

The absence of discrimination doesn't guarantee that a battered woman wins; men have been losing for years, when it was the fiancée and not the wife. The rules may feel harsh to the individual who is doing the best she can, but so do limits on the insanity defense, and the requirement that words are not enough to provoke. *Sometimes doing the best you can is not good enough for the rest of us,* and that is a judgment we are entitled to make, provided we make it in good faith.

Most battered women don't need separate rules anyway; they don't need Lenore Walker. The reason battered women's evidence is so widely accepted is because of the very political strength of the movement that supports it. Most battered women do not in fact kill husbands when they are asleep, Holly Maguigan found after an extensive study of all the appellate cases. They kill in fights. The main problem with the common law rules, Professor Maguian argues, is a problem of applying those rules fairly.[9]

White men still dominate law enforcement and the judiciary, although substantial progress has been made. Still, more women are decision makers in the criminal justice system than defendants; juries are very often predominantly female. More important, the purpose of inclusiveness should not be to build enough political strength for a separate set of rules. It is to be part of the process of defining and enforcing common standards. Husbands shouldn't kill wives. Wives shouldn't kill husbands.

Consider again the case of Avena Wanrow, the mother whose killing of an alleged child abuser led to the first explicit judicial recognition of the sexism of the reasonable man. What I have never understood, in the many years I have taught this case, is why she was convicted of murder in the first place. A mother killing a child abuser, a venereal disease spreader no less, in the middle of the night, convicted of murder? Ellie Nesler, who killed her son's alleged abuser while he was shackled in the courtroom, was only convicted of manslaughter. Where could you find twelve people to convict a mother of murder for killing a child abuser in these circumstances? It's not a hard case, even under traditional criminal law doctrine. You get all the child abuse history into evidence, on the grounds that it is directly relevant to her belief in the imminence of deadly force and to the reasonableness of that belief. The relative sizes and strengths of the two people have always been taken into account in evaluating the reasonableness of one's recourse to deadly force. Physical handicaps always get considered.

So why did the jury convict? The sexism in the instructions, which the court relied upon in reversing, seems the least persuasive explanation. A mother protecting her young? What could be a more conventionally acceptable reason for deadly force, even in the old common law days? It goes back as far as the jealous-husband defense. You couldn't find a sexist man alive who doesn't think his wife should kill the SOB. And this woman is on crutches, to boot.

Race? That is what Mrs. Wanrow's lawyers have on occasion suggested—that she was convicted because she was a Native American, that she was the victim of a discriminating jury. Did racism trump sexism?

The only clue to the jury's thinking is their request, during deliberations, to have the 911 tape replayed. Mrs. Wanrow's attorneys had tried without success at trial to have the tape excluded. In her conversation with the 911 operator, Mrs. Wanrow coolly reports the killing: "I shot him twice. I shot him with a .25 automatic." It is possible that the jury just didn't buy the argument that Mrs. Wanrow shot because she was afraid or startled; they listened to her voice, her description, the testimony offered by everybody, and believed that she shot to kill. If that is the case, second-degree murder—nonpremeditated killing—is a perfectly acceptable application of common law to fact. Provided, of course, that men in similar situations would be treated the same way.

TWO

Send Them a Message

The idea of the jury as an institution that is above politics is cherished by most Americans. But, like the "objective" common law, it is an impossibility. The jury is the human embodiment of the idea of the reasonable person. Juries have always been possessed of the power not only to enforce the law but also to decide not to. The ability of the jury to acquit a guilty man and thus nullify the law is a safeguard of liberty when rarely used, and an invitation to anarchy when used too often. The question, as always, is how we do our politics.

"Send them a message," Johnny Cochran implored the Simpson jury in his final argument. The message he wanted them to send was a protest of racism. "If you don't do it, who will?" The tool he was urging them to use was the power of acquittal. The argument that jurors should use their power to acquit a guilty man in order to protest a racist system is the mirror image of the assault on the reasonable man addressed in Chapter 1. Advocates of jury nullification argue that the system is inherently racist, and that the answer is to nullify the law rather than to work even harder to enforce it fairly. The power to acquit a guilty man, professor and former prosecutor Paul Butler argues, "is perhaps the only legal power black people have to escape the tyranny of the majority."[1]

"Could you have voted to convict a man who you believed was guilty, if you also believed that police officers had deliberately planted evidence against him? Did the jurors who voted to acquit on the basis of these beliefs violate their oaths and act improperly?" So asks a full-page advertisement for Professor Dershowitz's eloquent effort to justify the Simpson verdict. His argument in *Reasonable Doubts* is not that O. J. Simpson is innocent but that the jury was right to acquit even if it thought Simpson guilty, in order to protest police lying and racism. "I am confident," Professor Dershowitz writes, "that the jury's unanimous acquittal in this case will promote truth in the long run, by sending a powerful message that business as usual will not always be tolerated."[2]

The criminal trials that have defined not only Los Angeles in the 1990s but the nation as a whole are easier for many of us to understand as political statements than as applications of law to facts. The Simi Valley jury's acquittal of the four police officers charged with beating Rodney King and the verdicts that acquitted Damian Williams of the most serious charges arising out of his near-murder of Reginald Denny, the white trucker beaten on the eve of the Los Angeles riots, make more sense as political judgments than as factual or evidentiary ones. The most generous thing that can be said of these juries is not that they think it's reasonable to beat up people of a different race—not that they think smashing a man's head with a brick, which is what Damian Williams did, is not a deadly threat to him—but that they were addressing altogether different issues. The Simi Valley verdict can be seen as a message of support to the police department, in much the same way the Simpson jury can be read as a vote of no-confidence. The Damian Williams verdict is understandable as a call for a truce, not a judgment about the lethal potential of bricks or the acceptability of nearly killing innocent white people. In each case, acquittal can be seen as a political decision to flout the law.

Nor is the phenomenon limited to high-profile cases. Anecdotal reports confirm the accounts of police and prosecutors, who say that the cases that used to be the easiest are now the hardest. In Washington, D.C., where Mayor Marion Barry was acquitted of 13 out of 14 counts, notwithstanding videotape showing him smoking crack cocaine, nearly 30 percent of all felony trials result in acquittal. In Detroit the numbers have been higher still, more than twice the national average. In the South Bronx, as many as 47 percent of black defendants are acquitted, according to 1996 reports. While jury trials remain the exception rather than the rule, three strikes and mandatory drug sentencing laws increase the defendant's incentive to request a trial, and the perception that these laws are unfair to blacks, not to mention disproportionate in their punishment regardless of race, increase the jury's incentive to acquit. Prosecutors report that they are increasingly losing cases where they must rely on the testimony of police officers, particularly white officers, in front of black juries, while two national studies released in 1996 found that black defendants who go to trial are in fact convicted less often for crimes of violence than white defendants.[3]

The possibility of jury nullification is built into the jury system, and is integral to it. Our system is structured to protect against a jury that goes wrong by convicting an innocent man. Our standards of proof require that when there is reasonable doubt of guilt, the case must be resolved in favor of the defendant. The judge has a right to throw out a case even before giving it to the jury if he doesn't think the burden of proof has been met. And a conviction can be reversed if higher courts believe it wrong.

But there's no stopping a jury that decides to let a guilty man go free. The prosecution cannot appeal acquittals. Double jeopardy bars retrial, unless a federal law has also been violated. The power to refuse to enforce the law remains in the hands of jurors for the very practical reason that acquittals are final.

This is not a technical glitch in the system, merely an undesirable side effect of the rules relating to double jeopardy. The jury system took root in America, first and foremost, not because it was or is a superior means of finding facts but as a check against the abuse of political power. "A right to jury trial," the Supreme Court held in *Duncan v. Louisiana* (1968), "is granted to criminal defendants in order to prevent oppression by the Government." The founders saw in the right to jury trial protection against overzealous prosecutors and judges "too responsive to the voice of higher authority." The "fear of unchecked power, so typical of our State and Federal Governments in other respects, found expression in the criminal law in this insistence upon community participation in the determination of guilt or innocence."

This fear of unchecked power encompassed not only the need to protect the innocent but also the concern that government would seek to enforce unjust laws. One of the best-known instances of jury nullification was the refusal of a colonial jury to enforce the seditious libel law against John Peter Zenger, who had written and published articles critical of the British. The colonies' experience with unjust British law led a number of the new states, in their state constitutions, explicitly to empower juries to decide the law. For much of the nineteenth century, in contrast with the English system, American juries were instructed that it was their right to decide not only whether the defendant committed the wrongs alleged but also whether the law under which he was being prosecuted was just and whether he should be punished. Or as one juror put it after the judge had stated the law: "Is that ur law, or just what you say ur law is?"

But as American law evolved, and as fear of central authority decreased, the English view of juries took hold here as well. Affording juries the power to refuse to enforce unjust laws protects us against tyranny, but if they use that power too often, we end up with anarchy instead. The issue reached the Supreme Court in 1895, and in a famous opinion by the first Justice Harlan, the Court ruled against the right of jury nullification. The case involved a murder at sea. The defendants, it appears, had no defense except to try (and fail) to exclude incriminatory evidence and to hope for sympathy from the jury. Today, they might have an expert on "seamen's syndrome" but in *Sparf and Hansen* (1895) all of the evidence was put on by the government. The Court, over the defense's objection, told the jury that "it may be in the *power* of the jury under the indictment by which these defendants are accused and tried of finding them guilty of a less crime than murder, to wit, manslaughter, or an attempt to commit murder; *yet as I have said in this case, if a felonious homicide has been committed at all, of which I repeat you are the judges, there is nothing to reduce it below the grade of murder.*" During deliberations, a juror requested further instructions, specifically asking about the possibility of some verdict other than guilty of murder, or not guilty.

Juror: Then there is no other verdict we can bring in except guilty or not guilty?
Court: In a proper case, a verdict for manslaughter may be rendered, as the district attorney has stated; and even in this case you have the physical power to do so; but as one of the tribunals of the country, a jury is expected to be governed by law, and the law it should receive from the court.

The defendants were convicted of murder, and appealed. One of their grounds was that the trial judge had erred in telling the jury that it was bound to follow the law as stated by the judge and in excluding the right to consider manslaughter as a sort of compromise or sympathy verdict. A divided Supreme Court affirmed the convictions, disagreeing at length on the question whether a jury should be told that it was bound to follow the law. The dissent, relying on historical authority, invoked the jury's traditional role as the conscience of the community, and its roots in the framers' distrust of government. Justice Harlan, writing for the Court, cited his own history, emphasizing the importance of predictability and evenhandedness in the law. Quoting Justice Story, he asserted that "every person accused as a criminal has a right to be tried according to the law of the land, the fixed law of the land; and not by the law as the jury may understand it, or chose, from wantonness or ignorance or accidental mistake, to interpret it."

Justice Harlan certainly understood that nothing a judge said could actually take away the jury's power to nullify the law; indeed, the trial judge himself made that clear. But in denying that juries had that power as a matter of right, Harlan sought to limit as much as judges can the circumstances in which it would be used. "This so-called right of jury nullification is put forward in the name of liberty and democracy, but its explicit avowal risks the ultimate logic of anarchy," the United States Court of Appeals for the D.C. Circuit concluded in *United States v. Malone* (1972) over Chief Judge Bazelon's dissent. The Court of Appeals in this ruling held that Vietnam War protestors at Dow Chemical Company had no right to an instruction informing the jury of its power to acquit notwithstanding the law and the evidence. The legal system, in not informing the jury of the power it has, "is not being duplicitous, chargeable with chicane and intent to deceive." The limitation on information is "a governor to avoid excess; the prerogative is reserved for the exceptional case."

Does racism pose such an exceptional case? In California, 40 percent of black men between the ages of 20 and 30 are convicted criminals. Nationally, more black men go to prison than to college; less than 10 percent of the college population in America, and nearly 50 percent of the prison population, consists of black men. More blacks are in prison in America than whites, even though blacks comprise only 12 percent of the population. In the first year of its enforcement, 43 percent of the third-strikers in California were black. In 1995 the Sentencing Project—a group, based in Washington, D.C., that focuses on alternative sentencing—reported that 30 percent of all black men between the ages of 20 and 30 in America were either in prison, on probation, or on parole. Experts predict that this number could rise to 50 percent in coming years. In New York, 25 percent of the population is composed of African-Americans and Hispanics but they represent 83 percent of that state's inmate population. Hispanics are over-represented, but the disparity is greatest among blacks.[4]

The traditional argument that the system is racist points to these figures, standing alone, as proof of bias. But virtually every expert agrees that the rate of incarceration in the criminal justice system roughly matches the rate of offending. More blacks are locked up because they commit more of the crimes that land people in prison. It's true that crack cocaine, more likely to be used by blacks, is punished far more severely than powdered cocaine, a disparity which is regularly attacked as racist, as is the concentration of drug enforcement efforts in the inner city. But both policies are also explainable in non-racist terms. The violent crime problem, U.S. Attorney Nora Manella argues, "is among the inner city street gangs, not the suburban bowling leagues and women's bridge clubs." Crack dealers and users tend to have longer and more serious criminal records than cocaine users and are more likely to be carrying a weapon when arrested. Referring to the wealthy neighborhoods of Southern California, Manella argues, "There's no evidence that Bel Air or Brentwood or Palos Verdes is ravaged by rampant drug-related violence. If it were, we'd be there."

Indeed, a system that didn't take crack seriously and didn't concentrate its efforts on those areas where drugs wreak the greatest havoc would itself be open to attack as racist, and the failure of Congress to move on the Sentencing Commission's recommendation that the disparity between crack and powder be eliminated owes more to political cowardice than to racism. Moreover, even if you remove crack from the equation, even if you remove all drug offenses, you still end up with a disproportionate number of minorities in prison for crimes of violence. And it's not because the system convicts them more often than it does whites; quite the opposite is true, in fact, for all crimes of violence.

The most troubling aspect of the argument, though, is that the price of simplistically equating black incarceration with racism is to ignore the victims of most minority crime: other minorities. For all the fears fanned of interracial crime, the reality is that most crime is a local, intraracial phenomenon. Those who would deny the reality of black crime also deny the reality of black victimization.

The existence of a statistical correlation between race and crime doesn't for a moment prove a causal effect. It doesn't prove that race has anything to do with causing crime. But the whole array of factors that do contribute to the likelihood of criminal behavior—single-parent families, drug use, working for drug traffickers, poverty, lack of opportunity, a culture of violence, easy access to guns, the presence and influence of gangs—correlates with race in America. While the black middle-class is growing, the black underclass is sinking.

"Put in the starkest terms," Professor Orlando Patterson writes, "the bottom third of the African American population—some 10 million persons—live in dire poverty while the bottom 10 percent or so—the so-called underclass—exist in an advanced stage of social, economic, and moral disintegration."[5] More black children live only with their mother than with both parents. In the District of Columbia, where a majority of every department in the criminal justice system is composed of blacks, 41 percent of black men in their 20s are in prison, on probation, or on parole.

That makes racism inevitable. We are all racists when it comes to crime, and so is the system, albeit not in the simplistic sense that critics of incarceration rates presume. The standards of judgment that define the procedural steps from investigation to conviction—reasonable suspicion for a stop, probable cause for a search, reasonable doubt for conviction—are not mathematical measures. Decision making doesn't work that way. Does anyone doubt that black men are viewed with greater suspicion by police? If we start out believing that blacks are more likely to be criminals, how can it not be easier to decide that there is reasonable suspicion? If we start out believing that too many white police officers and departments are tainted by racism, how can it not be easier to see incompetence as reasonable doubt?

The Beverly Hills Police Department is considered to be one of the best in California. It has always engaged in a version of proactive, community-based policing. Police officers enforce loitering laws, stop strangers, use traffic laws as an occasion to ask questions. The department is currently being sued for race discrimination. The plaintiffs are a collection of middle-class law-abiding black men—a salesman picking up his wife for lunch, the captain of the high school football team, the handyman at a local church—who allege that they have been stopped repeatedly, searched, even (in the case of the handyman) wrestled to the ground in front of parishioners. Even stout defenders of the police acknowledge that an unknown black man in the neighborhood arouses greater citizen concern than a white man. Police are no doubt more likely to be summoned, or to intervene on their own, if it is a black stranger. When the police do intervene, they will take greater safety precautions in dealing with the black man, and they will not be surprised if he turns out to resist, to be armed. The police will protect themselves on the presumption that he is potentially dangerous.

Should we blame them? I ask my law school class at the University of Southern California, "How many of you have ever been stopped in Beverly Hills?" One white student raises her hand, a woman who went down a one-way street the wrong way and talked her way out of a ticket. Five of six black men raise their hands. The sixth doesn't have a car and never goes to Beverly Hills. One of the five, big and strapping, with a new Jeep, says he is stopped regularly—a black man, driving a fancy car during daylight hours, not obviously employed. He thought about it before he bought the car but decided he really wanted it anyway. So he keeps his license and registration handy. Often, he says, he can see the police officer's hand reaching for his gun as he approaches him. "Driving while black" is how Harvard Professor Henry Louis Gates describes the offense, nowhere spelled out in the statute books but regularly enforced across America.[6]

I look at my student carefully. Could I tell the difference between him, a member of the upper middle-class driving a new car while a first-year law student, and a drug dealer, a gang member? Would I get on an elevator alone with this man?

There are, still, too many Mark Fuhrmans. But my student wasn't stopped by a Mark Fuhrman. He doesn't think he was stopped because the cops were looking to hassle black men or because they hate black people. Once he showed his law school ID, they couldn't have been nicer, he says. Black women aren't complaining about Beverly Hills, so the issue isn't racism pure

up exclusively of one is different from a community composed of both; the subtle interplay of influences one on the other is among the imponderables. To insulate the courtroom from either may not in a given case make an iota of difference. Yet a flavor, a distinct quality is lost if either sex is excluded. The exclusion of one may indeed make the jury less representative of the community than would be true if an economic or racial group were excluded.

Twenty-six years later, in holding unconstitutional a system for selecting the pool of potential jurors which systematically discriminated against blacks, Justice Marshall, writing for the plurality of the Court, struck a similar theme in *Peters v. Kiff*:

> When any large and identifiable segment of the community is excluded from jury service, the effect is to remove from the jury room qualities of human nature and varieties of human experience, the range of which is unknown and perhaps unknowable. It is not necessary to assume that the excluded group will consistently vote as a class in order to conclude, as we do, that its exclusion deprives the jury of a perspective on human events that may have unsuspected importance in any case that may be presented.

Even Chief Justice Burger, in dissenting from the Court's ruling, recognized that "juries should not be deprived of the insights of the various segments of the community, for the 'common sense judgment of a jury' referred to in *Duncan v. Louisiana* is surely enriched when all voices can be heard."

"To acknowledge that jurors enter the jury room with views and values shaped in part by their creed, race or gender is not to accuse the jurors of bias in need of silencing," Professor Jeffrey Abramson argues eloquently. "It is to treasure the particularly rich conversations a democratic assembly inspires, precisely because it brings into one communal conversation persons from different sub-communities."[8] The difference between a needed perspective and an unfair bias is what you do with it once you're there.

A traditional legal-process answer to the reality of racism in the criminal justice system is to assure that juries are indeed representative, and then to scrutinize strictly racial stereotypes that may make it too easy to reach judgments, particularly about guilt. The way you make sure you're not discriminating against the black applicant is to look at him individually, judge him based on his qualifications, not a stereotype about blacks being less qualified. The way to avoid convicting someone for being a black man is to make judgments solely on the basis of the evidence presented. We pay attention to race to ensure that racism does not define our judgment.

The argument for race-based jury nullification proceeds on directly contrary premises, however. It calls on jurors to disregard the evidence of an individual's guilt, rather than looking only at that evidence, and to focus instead on the evidence of racism. "Considering the costs of law enforcement to the black community and the failure of white lawmakers to come up with any solutions to black antisocial conduct other than incarceration, it is, in fact, the moral responsibility of black jurors to emancipate some guilty black outlaws." The rule of law, Paul Butler argues, "is a myth, or at least not valid for African-Americans," given the instances in the past in which blacks have been denied its benefits. As for the argument that jury nullification is antidemocratic, Professor Butler asserts that "this is precisely why many African Americans endorse it."[9]

Professor Butler was surprised to find that most of his black colleagues in the very office that was prosecuting Mayor Marion Barry were rooting for his acquittal as a protest against racism. Many of my black students, who understood very clearly everything that was wrong with the O. J. Simpson case, were nonetheless cheering that a black man was standing up to a bad system. If twelve people, by virtue of serving on a jury, for once have power to stand up and say that enough is enough, why shouldn't they use it? Why *not* send a message?

Ultimately, it is a political question, requiring a political answer: It simply won't work. It can't be limited. It's a political disaster, sure to contribute to balkanization rather than to address it. It will lead to more crime, not less. It distorts the political debate, providing a ready excuse to ignore everything else. In refusing to see the jury room as a temple where we come together as a community to enforce our common law, jury nullification becomes a self-fulfilling prophecy of the impossibility of common law. As a political solution, it fails to advance the legitimate goals of those in whose name it is advanced, and in the long run it is likely to leave them worse off, not better.

In our politics, one group's assertion of a right to its own standards inevitably leads to others' demanding the same. Are blacks the only ones facing last resorts? Why not strike a blow for the women's community? While substantial progress has been made, gender bias remains an issue in the courts; domestic violence is still not being fully addressed. Men are still getting away with murder; why shouldn't women? Why not use Lorena Bobbitt to send a message that we're mad as hell, and they'd best pay attention?

What about the people who follow the law? Doesn't anyone understand that we are sick and tired of thugs ruling the roost? If your first reaction to the news that a citizen had killed a tagger was "Good for him," then you're engaged in jury nullification as well—as a member of the population that could never produce a jury that would convict. Imaginary juries nullify more laws than real ones.

And so it goes. Name your cause. If a syndrome doesn't save you, if the evidence of guilt is still too great, you can always turn it into a political message. These are extraordinary times in the Korean community; they are extraordinary times for Native Americans, gay Americans, religious Americans, even for white men. Blacks claim they have it worse—when it comes to crime, I'd argue they do—but they are unlikely to convince others under assault of that: the difference, at best, is one of degree. A balkanized polity will surely demand the perverse equality of irresponsibility: that is the lesson of the explosion of syndrome defenses. An eye for an eye will leave all of us blind.

And less safe. Particularly blacks. If you release drug dealers to the streets, the kids they are most likely to prey on are their black neighbors. If you pit the community against the system, the community loses. During the 1950s and 1960s, the racist exercise of police discretion was a major factor in a wide range of judicial rulings invalidating loitering laws, throwing out coerced confessions, requiring warnings before interrogation, establishing formulaic guidance for stops and searches, and excluding illegally seized evidence. One consequence of those efforts was to encourage police to get off the beat, get into cars two by two, and go only where invited, measuring their effectiveness according to the speed of their response. "Response times" went down, but that hardly matters in the bulk of cases, where the crime is already complete when the police are called.

Community-based policing is an effort to reinstate the best of traditional, discretionary, proactive policing, without the worst of the racism. Brilliantly rehabilitated as a nonracist crime-fighting approach by Professors James Q. Wilson and George Kelling in the 1980s, community policing operates on the premise that police officers can and should enforce norms of conduct in the community; that quality-of-life offenses which would traditionally be ignored, such as breaking windows in abandoned buildings, particularly in the poor neighborhoods where they are commonplace, should instead be vigorously addressed; that doing so will at the very least make neighborhoods seem safer, itself a plus; and that they should also become safer as a result, which experience suggests they do.[10]

Community policing is not a panacea; it hasn't worked everywhere. It takes time to change the culture of a police department. Still, the results have been promising. In New York City, under the leadership of William Bratton, a committed practitioner of community policing, crime decreased significantly across the board, and across-the-board reductions help communities that are hardest hit most.

The key to community policing is trust between the community and the police department. It is what makes the 90s version different from the 50s version. The way to avoid treating people like racial stereotypes is to have cops who know kids individually. People in the community know the difference between the football captain and the gang leader, and so should the police. The police department helps get abandoned buildings boarded up and abandoned cars removed. Jury nullification is a political step in the opposite direction—a reaffirmation of the adversarial relationship between the minority community and the police, in the form of a message of distrust.

Worse, the message is sent in the least persuasive form possible. Experience with the judicially imposed exclusionary rule makes clear everything that is wrong with doing politics by letting guilty people go free. In the three decades since *Mapp* was decided, the courts, in their efforts to avoid freeing the guilty in circumstances where, however fortuitously, the police turned out to be right, have repeatedly narrowed the scope of the Fourth Amendment's protections, blinked at deception, and rewritten facts. The exclusionary rule does encourage police officers to lie, as Alan Dershowitz has often charged, but they don't lie to frame the innocent. Police officers lie to explain why they went to the *right* house, searched the *right* guy, were right about where the gun was. All the incentives push the police to lie so that a criminal will not be freed; and if the judge calls them on it, he becomes the villain who let the bad guy out. While the reality is that exclusion is rare, the perception is that judicial protection of privacy is a major obstacle to crime control.

In politics, she who asks the question generally wins. The goal is to fight on your terms—which means to frame the question so that more people agree with your position than the other side's. The easiest way to lose a debate about police racism is to turn it into a fight about O. J. Simpson. If you're trying to protect young black men from police harassment, why do it by defending one of the very few whose celebrity transcended race? There must be a better way to get help for battered women than by defending the one in a million who hires a hit man to kill her spouse. The easiest way to lose a debate about domestic violence is to have to defend Lorena Bobbitt.

Jury nullification is a political boomerang. It turns legitimate complaints into marginal positions, allowing those who are supposed to be getting the message to focus on how outrageous it is that a guilty man or woman has gone free, and to avoid entirely the underlying grievances against the system.

Jury nullification also invites attacks on the jury system itself. Many historians believe that Justice Harlan saved the jury system when he restricted their stated role to applying the law and not making it. Every time a high-profile criminal walks, or a jury hangs on an abuse excuse, or acquits against the evidence, a politician somewhere gets on his soapbox to argue that we don't live by the law anymore. We take to our separate camps. We view each other with suspicion. Ambitious politicians dream up new initiatives to eliminate the requirement of unanimous juries. If juries see themselves as political tools, why shouldn't others? Jury nullification, magnified by the media coverage it receives, becomes another reason to lose faith in our ability to find common ground and trust in the rule of law.

The idea of common law demands that our decisions ultimately be explainable to ourselves and to each other in reasons that reach beyond race. That is no easy thing in a multicultural society. Not everyone sees the O. J. Simpson verdict as a case of jury nullification, including the jurors themselves. They claim they acquitted because they had reasonable doubt as to Simpson's guilt, and many commentators have charged that characterizing the jury's verdict as political is itself a racist reaction. The claim that their verdict was reasonable was also made by the Simi Valley jurors, who resented the charge that it was based on race and not facts.

In a diverse society, there are bound to be occasions where verdicts of reasonable doubt reached in good faith are wrongly perceived by others as intentional instances of jury nullification. We can do our best to explain verdicts to one another, but the system cannot close the gaps of society, much less turn inevitably political lines into something else. Even without Professor Butler and a name for it, there are bound to be instances where jury decisions leave some of us shaking our head. But that is all the more reason to follow Justice Harlan's lead in structuring the system to make jury nullification less rather than more likely, to treat it as an unstated exception rather than to embrace it as a call to arms.

The jury system is in desperate need of reform for reasons that go beyond the dangers of racism and jury nullification. The loss of confidence in juries is plainly part of a larger pattern in which our confidence in social institutions of all sorts has declined. We are becoming a nation of nonbelievers and nonparticipants in our civic religion. In the case of juries, it is not that we trust our government more than our forefathers did, but that we trust one another even less.

A poll in Los Angeles county taken as jury selection got under way in the Simpson case found that going into the trial, a majority of the respondents had "only some or very little" confidence in the ability of juries to decide criminal cases fairly. The major flaws volunteered by the respondents were incompetent jurors and failure to set aside prejudices and preconceived notions. Blacks had even less confidence in juries than whites. Even more troubling, a majority of those polled— 57 percent—for all their criticism of others, said they regarded jury service as a "personal choice," while only 41 percent saw it as a civic responsibility.[11]

Not long ago, a top Hollywood executive was going to be on jury duty. She had not sought an excuse, which was readily available at the time. She was going to the courthouse every day, and told colleagues that she found it satisfying. It was in the news because it was viewed as a sign that her days in her job must be numbered. Three weeks later, she was replaced. Juries cannot be representative if those with better things to do are routinely exempt, and both prosecutors and defense counsel are free to manipulate the selection process in the hopes of stacking the deck. No reason other than serious illness should exempt a person from jury service. If it's important, we should treat it as important. Our rules communicate our values.

The first twelve people who are qualified should serve. Qualified means that they don't have any personal knowledge of the case, and that the judge is satisfied that they understand the responsibilities of a juror and are capable of executing them. Certainly questions must be asked, particularly in high-profile cases, to assure that jurors have not already reached a judgment. But the purpose of questioning is to determine whether a juror can keep his mind open, not whether his is the kind of mind the defense or the prosecution particularly likes.

"Have you ever written a letter to the editor of a newspaper or magazine?" potential jurors in the Simpson case were asked. "Do you believe it is immoral or wrong to do an amniocentesis to determine whether a fetus has a genetic defect?" How was that relevant to anyone's ability to serve on the O. J. Simpson jury? The technical answer is that some jury consultant somewhere had found a correlation between the way some or all people answer these questions and potential attitudes toward issues or defenses in the case. Either that jury consultant is wrong, in which case we're wasting time and undermining confidence, or he's right, in which case we are allowing juries to be manipulated for the benefit of rich defendants and the likely detriment of the rule of law. Why should we tolerate either?

Studies on the civil side have shown jury consultants to have very limited impact. But the very idea that juror attitudes should be prescreened conflicts with the function of a jury as a place where diverse approaches and experiences—even, maybe especially, the racist ones—come together to be sorted out. Why in the world should the majority that wants juries to find facts and reflect common values allow either side to play politics with the selection process in the hopes of finding a jury that will be less likely to do either?

No one should be struck for no reason at all. Peremptory challenges, as Professor Nancy Marder has argued, interfere with the jury's performance of its public functions of finding facts and expressing public values.[12] The best that can be said for them is that they give the parties more control over jury selection, which serves the function of the jury as a protector of parties' rights. But it serves it too well. Let me choose the electorate and I can win any election. What does that prove? The Supreme Court has held that peremptory challenges cannot be exercised to discriminate on the basis of race or gender, but violations are almost impossible to prove. If I am allowed to exclude someone for no reason at all, how can you prove that I did it because of race? Not easily. But there is an alternative to a test that can't be met. Why excuse anyone from jury service for no reason at all?

The question is not whether the jury is free from politics but whether it is a political idea that is worth preserving and safeguarding. If it is, then we should protect it from those who would use it as a means and not respect it as an end.

THREE

The Long Shadow of Willie Horton

The best that can be said of the political debate about crime in America is that it has nothing to do with crime. Politically speaking, crime is a values issue; the value is toughness. You can't be too tough, but you can get clobbered for being too soft. The problem with this kind of debate is not that it cost my liberal friends their political futures; Bill Clinton figured out the answer to that. Today, Democrats outdo themselves to prove that they are just as tough as Republicans. Everyone has learned the lesson of Willie Horton. No one tells the truth, and the political dishonesty is distorting and destroying the system.

Willie Horton is the most famous criminal in American politics, a black first-degree murderer who, while on a weekend furlough from a Massachusetts penal institution, brutally raped a Maryland woman in her home. Michael Dukakis, the 1988 Democratic nominee for President, was the governor of Massachusetts at the time Horton was furloughed. As governor, he defended the policy of furloughing first-degree murderers even after Horton's crime, and he refused to meet with a delegation, including the victim and her family, who had come to Massachusetts to protest that policy. It was a major issue for Dukakis as governor, and while there is a near-mythic tale about its discovery by the Republicans in a New Jersey focus group, the truth is that everyone knew it was coming, even if we could never agree on how to handle it.

"I'll turn Willie Horton into your running mate," Lee Atwater, George Bush's campaign manager, promised in the spring of 1988, when a virtually unknown Dukakis was still riding high in the polls. Atwater did, and later said on his deathbed that he regretted it. Dukakis's tendency to see issues in terms of policy rather than symbol made it even easier. When asked about Horton, Dukakis would explain the rationale for furlough policies, which played into the Republican hand. On another occasion, he proudly asserted himself a card-carrying member of the ACLU, and the Republicans never let him forget it. In the final presidential debate, in response to Bernard Shaw's version of the Willie Horton question—what would you do if your wife were raped?—Dukakis responded by reiterating his opposition to the death penalty. "Willie Horton" is political shorthand for being soft on crime, for being on the side of the criminal, for not empathizing with or sharing the values of average Americans. It is shorthand for political death, even without the racial overtones.

And there were racial overtones. Willie Horton surely would have been an issue had he been white, but would it have been as effective? There were never-ending debates on the Democratic side about how to handle the racial aspects of Willie Horton. Do you accuse the other side of using race-laden symbols and pouring gas on the flames of racism? Or will that cost you even more votes? Will people think you're even softer on crime by seeming to defend the criminal instead of attacking him? The argument raged back and forth; the more things got divided along lines of race, the worse our numbers looked in the South. That's the piece of the Willie Horton strategy that I think Lee Atwater regretted.

It was in Baltimore, in 1989, at a forum at Johns Hopkins University, that I finally disposed of the Willie Horton question once and for all. "What should Governor Dukakis have done about Willie Horton?" a young woman asked me from the back of the room. Kept him in prison, I answered. That's it. Everyone laughed, except Ed Rollins, my Republican counterpoint for the evening. Willie Horton is an easy question.

What should we do with Willie Horton? Lock him up. Should a man who rapes while out on furlough have been furloughed? Obviously not. The system failed. It doesn't matter what race he is. It doesn't even matter if it was a good program that failed. Why are we debating this? This is a debate only one side can win.

The traditional structure of the liberal–conservative crime debate is a debate between punishment and rehabilitation, between their responsibility for breaking the law and our responsibility for creating a rotten society. It is a debate you don't hear very much, except when conservative talk show hosts are debating themselves, for the very simple reason that the liberal position is politically untenable. You can't get elected if you take that position, for good reason, I think. Most people who grow up in our society, however rotten it is, don't rape and rob and kill other people. Those who do deserve to be punished for it. Whether they are capable of being rehabilitated is much debated, but it is certainly not something "we" owe "them." Committing a crime shouldn't get you to the front of the line for a job; not committing a crime should. A major reason a generation of liberals didn't see it that way was race.

In 1980, in the meetings I went to as a Democratic staffer on the Senate Judiciary Committee, the issue of crime was always intertwined with the issue of race. I remember well one meeting, where I was selling the idea of "security" as one of those unifying themes that we are always looking for in politics. I had economic security, national security, and of course, personal security. Crime. One of my most respected colleagues looked at me with horror, and explicitly accused me of racism. You want us to take the lead in locking up black men? he asked me. Everyone else in the meeting now looked at me with horror, too. Yes. White people, too. If they're rapists and killers. Help the victims, not the bad guys.

In our history, racism has clearly made it too easy to convict people. But it can also make it too hard. The injuries of racism are real. But so are the injuries of crime. The man who raped me when I was 21 deserved to be punished without regard to race or racism. Whatever happened to him in his life, he was still responsible for what he did to me. That much, at least, I always knew.

No issue has captured the liberal dilemma better than the death penalty. All of the candidates I worked for, all of the professors who taught me, were against the death penalty; some of them considered it barbaric and unconstitutional on its face; all of them considered it racist in its imposition. That is how I was brought up, legally speaking. In rape law, where I did my own work, there is a long and terrible tradition of punishing black men with death for raping white women, in some cases on very dubious proof. Indeed, race continues to play a role in the imposition of the death penalty; murderers (black or white) who kill white people are more likely to be executed than those who kill blacks.

But that argument failed to persuade a majority of the Supreme Court, not to mention most Americans. It doesn't even persuade me anymore. Why should the statistical undervaluation of the lives of black victims provide the grounds for reversal in the case of an unquestionably guilty and brutal killer?

The statistics, on closer examination, in fact present a mixed picture. While it is true that killers of whites are more likely to be executed, it is also true that white murderers are substantially more likely to be executed than black murderers, because most murders are intraracial.

In 1988 then-Governor Bill Clinton came to Boston to participate in presidential debate preparations. During one of the breaks, after a long and frustrating session of Willie-Horton/pledge-of-allegiance/ACLU/death-penalty questions, the future President explained crime politics to me. He took out a piece of paper, and on one side listed the Democratic governors who were for the death penalty, and on the other those who were against. It was a breakdown between the past and the future, politically speaking. During the 1992 campaign, then-candidate Clinton flew back to Arkansas to sign the death warrant for a mentally impaired man, a decision viewed by many as a sign of his determination to avoid any soft-on-crime issue. Two years later, he decided to abandon the judicial nomination of Peter Edelman, a friend and the husband of an even closer friend, after Republican conservatives made clear that they would use Edelman's release of a killer to a half-way house (while Edelman was a New York State official in the 1970s) to argue that he was too liberal. Willie Horton was explicitly invoked.

The more executions there are, the more likely it is that someday there will be a mistake. Are we willing to accept that risk? What are we willing to do to guard against it? Justice Stevens, who during my clerkship year considered and denied a stay of execution for the first man executed against his will in two decades, signaling the end of the moratorium on involuntary executions, told me recently that he has now come to doubt the capacity and the willingness of the system to provide the level of fairness that a punishment of death requires. The American Bar Association has reached a similar conclusion. One legislator in Massachusetts even switched his vote on the death penalty after Louise Woodward's conviction. But in most of America, to express concern about the death penalty in any form is to make yourself unelectable. The question whether we are administering death fairly should not be a measure of toughness.

The price of seeing crime issues as a measure of toughness is not limited to capital cases. It is also paid by judges, and ultimately by taxpayers. Over the last two decades, getting "tough" on crime has meant the redistribution of decision-making power in the criminal justice system from the least politicized decision makers to the most; and from the most experienced to the least. What's worse, passing mandatory laws and stripping judges of discretion, as we have increasingly done as an expression of toughness, is ultimately the way to let Willie Horton go free.

During the 1950s, Congress and many states passed laws setting mandatory five-year terms for drug distribution. But by the late 1960s, most of these laws had fallen into disfavor, victims of the then-prevailing view that the primary purpose of punishment was rehabilitation; that rehabilitation required individualized judgments as to when the inmate was ready to return to society; and that these judgments could and should be made by judges and parole boards operating with the broadest possible discretion. In practical terms, this philosophy translated into indeterminate sentencing. Statutes regularly authorized punishment for "any term of years," giving judges broad discretion to determine the sentence and allowing virtually any evidence to be considered in making this determination.

While the rehabilitation model gave judges almost unlimited discretion in making formal judgments about sentence, in most states the decision to release the offender was ultimately in the hands of a parole board, which would decide whether he had in fact been rehabilitated. In Massachusetts, for example, it used to be the case that any prisoner sentenced to a "Concord sentence" was immediately eligible for parole—even if he was sentenced to ten or fifteen years. If a judge wanted a defendant to serve at least one-half of his term, the judge had to impose a "Norfolk sentence." It was not uncommon for a victim or his family to sit in the back of a courtroom and hear an assailant sentenced to a term of five or ten years, only to learn that he had been released a few months later.

This sentencing system came under attack from both right and left. Liberals attacked the disparity in sentences imposed on criminals who had been convicted of the same crime, with particular concern about alleged racial disparities. Conservatives took issue with the leniency and deceptions of the system. Liberals sought tougher sentences for white-collar crimes: why should minorities who stole in the streets be subject to harsher punishment than businessmen who stole in the boardroom? Conservatives sought tougher sentences for drug-related crime. In the 1983 debates about sentencing reform in the United States Senate, the consensus that there was too much disparity in criminal sentences crossed party and ideological lines.

At the same time, in academic circles, there was increasing support for presumptive sentencing models: systems that would establish ranges of permissible sentences for particular crimes, with the judge's discretion limited to choosing a sentence within the stated range, guided by predetermined criteria, such as the defendant's prior criminal record. Most presumptive sentencing models also included requirements that the defendant serve at least a certain percentage of his term— one-half or two-thirds was typical—before being eligible for parole. Some went so far as to eliminate parole altogether, requiring a defendant to serve the full stated sentence less only "good time" credit, earned for good behavior in prison and maintained to create incentives for discipline in prison. In order to protect elected officials from the need to approve sentencing guidelines that would be seen, politically, as far too short for the crimes charged—would any politician want to acknowledge that armed robbers should serve only a few years?—authority actually to set the guideline ranges was, in many such models, invested in independent commissions.

Academics tended to draw sharp distinctions between such presumptive schemes and mandatory sentencing models, which required a judge to impose a fixed term of years whenever a defendant was convicted of a specific crime. The academic argument was that punishment should be both offender-oriented and offense-oriented, and that mandatory models, by eliminating any offender characteristics from the imposition of sentence, veered too far in one direction. But in truth, the difference was only one of degree, and was probably too subtle in any event to play a major role in political debate.

If judges couldn't be trusted, why trust them with ranges? Why not just set the sentence by law? And so the legislature, duly composed of politicians, did—every election year. In 1984 Congress passed comprehensive sentencing reform which established a guidelines commission to set new ranges for all federal offenses, along with specific criteria limiting judges' discretion even within the presumptive ranges. Parole was effectively eliminated. Prosecutors were authorized for the first time to appeal sentences that fell short of the guidelines range. The champions of the bill, liberal and conservative, pointed to it as an answer to both the problems of disparity and the absence of truth-in-sentencing.

The same bill that created the guidelines commission also set mandatory minimum sentences for crimes committed with firearms, and set a 15-year mandatory minimum sentence for possession of a firearm by a person with three previous state or federal convictions for robbery or burglary. Defenders of the guidelines claim that it was the proliferation of mandatory sentences that undermined the workability of the guidelines. Take your pick as to which act of Congress to blame.

Every two years since, Congress has gotten even "tougher," adding new mandatory minimum provisions to the federal scheme and enhancing punishment for specific crimes. The 1986 bill imposed five- and ten-year mandatory minimum terms for drug-related crimes. In 1988 more drug-related crimes were added to the list. In 1990 savings and loan "kingpins" got a new federal mandatory minimum. In 1992 more mandatory minimums were proposed and approved but died amid pre-election controversy about changes in procedures for habeas corpus—changes now enacted as part of the 1996 legislation. In 1994 Congress, as part of a crime bill in which prevention programs became the subject of ridicule, added a long list of federal crimes to those for which a penalty of death could be imposed.

The move to mandatory terms and tougher punishment has dominated state politics as well. In the last twenty years, every state legislature has passed either mandatory sentencing laws or guidelines or both. The most recent national obsession has been with "three strikes and you're out." California, in mid-O. J., led the way, with the legislature passing five different versions of the law before the people followed suit. As drafted and enacted, the law did not require that the third felony be violent, nor did it take account of the time period between the felonies, nor did it allow for any judicial assessment of the dangerousness of the person committing the crimes. By the time of the election, even the father of Polly Klaas, whose brutal murder by Richard Alan Davis when she was twelve inspired the proposition, had come out against it. But every single candidate running for statewide office that November supported it, notwithstanding its flaws. Its primary sponsor, the father of another young woman slain by a three-time loser, would hear of no objections, and few were willing to tell the father of a murdered daughter that he was wrong. Even fewer were willing to trust the voters to understand that. Who wants to defend Willie Horton? The initiative passed, with 72 percent support.

The result of mandatory laws and punishment by slogan is that we spend more and more money locking up less and less violent people. At both the state and federal levels we have seen the biggest prison-building boom in history. State prison populations have increased more than 60 percent in five years. Today, one-and-a-half million Americans are behind bars. A report by the conservative Cato Institute concluded that the single biggest reason for our expanding prison population has been the decision to send to prison offenders who would otherwise have received an alternative sentence, most of them drug users. One out of five federal prisoners is in jail for what the Justice Department itself classifies as low-level activity, involving no violence, no serious prior criminal record, and no sophisticated activity.[1]

It is in the nature of any rule, even the most carefully thought out, to be over- and under-inclusive. Most states set the driving age at 16. Some kids are really mature enough at 15; some kids aren't ready until 17 or 18, but it's not the sort of judgment you can efficiently make case-by-case. And even if you tried in good faith, the result would almost surely be attacked as unfair and, these days, probably as discriminatory. So you pick an average that works best for the largest number of people and apply it across the board. In the case of sentencing, with Willie Horton breathing down our necks, we have set that average as high as we can: Every crack user gets punished as though he were a violent gang member. Every third-striker gets punished as though he were Polly Klaas's killer.

The results of the third-strike law are, on occasion, plainly ridiculous. There was the much-publicized pizza thief, an employed, engaged, almost middle-aged man who stole a piece of pepperoni pizza from another table on a dare and ended up in prison for life. Or the man who stole cologne from the drug store, or another who stole meat from the grocery store; both face life in prison. Or the 48-year-old longshoreman who gave the teenage boyfriend of a friend's daughter a ride to the Burger King and ended up in federal prison for ten years without parole for aiding and abetting the boy's drug deal. Ten years is twice the average time served in federal prison for robbery.

More often, the mandatory terms and life sentences end up being applied to drug users and thieves instead of dangerous predators. Upwards of 70 percent of the third strikes in the first two years of the California law's application have been nonviolent. Drug use is the most common third strike; nationally, nearly a third of those in prison are being held for drug offenses, as compared to less than 10 percent in 1980.[2]

It has been well established by criminologists that a small percentage of all criminals commit a disproportionate number of all crimes. Most criminals "age out" of crime as they get older, establish ties to the community, get married, have children. But there is a small percentage—what criminologists call the right tail of the right tail of the curve—who don't age out. They start out more violent, and stay that way. A pioneering study of boys born in Philadelphia found that 6 percent of the boys committed over half of the crimes committed by everyone in the cohort. This 6-percent rule was duplicated in further studies in Philadelphia and across the country. National surveys have found that 80 percent of all crimes are committed by about 20 percent of all criminals. A study in Orange County, California, over seven years found that 8 percent of juvenile delinquents commit about 55 percent of juvenile crimes, and more than half of these repeat offenders were arrested again after adulthood. In Los Angeles county, studies have found that 16 percent of all offenders are responsible for over half the repeat offenses.[3]

Politicians like to argue that these are the predators at whom the three strikes bills are aimed. They may be aimed at them, but they're missing the mark. Waiting until someone has been convicted three times by our inefficient criminal justice system means punishing too many older hapless criminals and too few of the young predators who pose the greatest threat. A Rand Corporation study found that the benefits of the three-strikes proposal, in crime-reduction terms, derived not from imprisoning third strikers but from lengthening the prison terms of second-time violators—a less-publicized part of the three-strikes package. They also found that any number of other measures for targeting high-risk offenders, including an individualized test that they came up with, would be more effective in cutting crime at lower cost.[4]

At the same time, the pressure such mandatory laws have put on the system is enormous. The more strictly these laws are enforced, the more defendants request jury trials, the longer the backlogs, the more crowded the prison system, the earlier people will in fact get out at the other end. As of 1990, almost forty states were under court order to relieve prison overcrowding by releasing prisoners. One in seven state facilities is overcrowded. In California, convicted prisoners in the county jail serve only 25 percent of their sentences because it is literally overflowing with people awaiting trial. Such revelations cause public outrage. The public doesn't understand that the partisan debate is meant to be symbolic; it was never expected to actually work. Or perhaps they do understand that, which is what breeds so much cynicism.

The worst of it is that treating petty thieves and drug users as if they were killers too often results in killers being treated too leniently. The Cato study concluded that mandatory sentences are in fact the best thing that ever happened to violent criminals (from the criminals' point of view), because overcrowding forces across-the-board early release. Time served for violent crimes has decreased with the explosion of mandatory drug minimums. In Florida, as the number of drug offenders serving longer sentences has increased, the average prison stay has dropped to 16 months. As Judge Lawrence Irving, a Reagan appointee who quit the bench in frustration over the sentencing laws, pointed out, "You've got murderers who get out sooner than some kid who did some stupid thing with drugs."[5]

Richard Alan Davis, on parole for a third offense when he kidnapped and killed Polly Klaas, is a case in point. Virtually everyone who dealt with Davis in the criminal justice system recognized him as a serious and violent predator who should be in prison both as punishment for his crimes and to protect the rest of us. But the legislature set him free, because mandatory terms also means mandatory release. Davis was in prison serving a six-month to life term for kidnapping. He'd already been turned down for parole three times. But when new mandatory sentence laws were passed, his indeterminate sentence was recalculated to a determinate length consistent with the average sentence to be imposed under the new, supposedly tougher, rules.

In Davis's case, those rules required him to serve 72 months—six years. Davis had already served six years. He was released right away. No judge or parole officer could stop it. Three years later, Davis kidnapped another woman. This time, he received the maximum determinate sentence of sixteen years. But the truth is that we don't have enough prisons for everyone who gets sixteen years to serve all sixteen. So California legislators, faced with bursting prisons, passed a law requiring all prisoners to serve one-half of their mandatory terms, effectively cutting them in half across the board. Davis was released, again automatically, in exactly eight years. Then he kidnapped Polly Klaas.

▼　　▼　　▼

Discretion in the criminal justice system is like toothpaste in a closed tube. Squeeze one end, and it ends up somewhere else. You don't get rid of it by moving it around; you just move it around. Discretion is the inevitable result of the system's need to be selective. The realities of limited space and limited resources mandate it. We simply don't have room in prisons for everyone the police bring in, much less everyone who commits crimes.

The Sentencing Project has calculated that for every crime committed, there is a 1 in 20 chance of going to prison. Other studies have put it at 1 in 100. The criminal justice system, as David Anderson aptly describes it, is a funnel, guided by the exercise of discretion.[6] The easiest way to get away with murder, or any other crime, is to be discreet enough not to be caught. Once caught, official discretion takes over. Does the officer detain you or let you walk? For what offense are you detained—weapons violation, driving to endanger, narcotics possession, murder? What does the prosecutor think about the chances of a conviction on the top count? What does she file? What plea is she willing to take?

What partisan politics has succeeded in doing is moving the discretion to make decisions about punishment from the judiciary and the parole boards to legislators and prosecutors. The result is that we have seemingly mandatory rules targeted at the worst offender, with the discretion to decide whether to apply them to everybody else placed solely in the hands of the prosecutor. The prosecutor decides what crimes to charge, what sentence to trigger. In the three-strikes scheme passed in California, the prosecutor decides whether the prior convictions count as strikes or don't count. In the federal system, prosecutors decide who gets credit for cooperating and what

▼

counts as substantial cooperation, which is in most cases the only permissible basis under the guidelines for judges to reduce a sentence.

In cases where the defendant pleads guilty, which is the overwhelming majority of cases, mandatory sentences turn the charging decision and the sentencing decision into one. It is hard to imagine anyone proposing that Americans should be sent to prison for life without a judge being involved. But in effect that is precisely what happens. Consider the procedure in Los Angeles County. Every crime that can be charged as a third strike is charged as a third strike, a policy which gives prosecutors enormous leverage in plea bargaining. Drug users and petty thieves routinely find themselves facing life sentences. The decision about what bargain to accept—whether to insist on life, or start discounting one or more of the strikes—rests in the sole, unreviewed, and unreviewable discretion of the deputy district attorneys who head the different offices. There is a weekly kaffeeklatsch among the deputies where they talk about whatever cases they choose to bring up, but no decisions are made there, and it is widely recognized that different deputies take different approaches, more and less willing to compromise. In one building, which houses offices serving two different areas, different standards apply on different floors.

In most offices, the deputy DA wouldn't charge the pizza thief. Maybe he was unlucky and wound up in the office nicknamed "No Walk." Maybe the prosecutor was trying to make a point, or was getting ready to challenge his boss for reelection. Maybe the owner of the pizza parlor was a major political contributor who wants to keep the riffraff out. Even at its best, prosecutorial discretion gets exercised invisibly.

Invisible discretion in a system still dominated by black defendants and white decision makers is bound to be attacked as racist, and it has been. In filings in federal court occasioned by a lawsuit challenging its enforcement policy as discriminatory, the United States Attorney's office in Los Angeles spelled out the factors they consider in deciding whether to charge crack as a federal offense: the amount of drugs involved, the presence or absence of firearms, and past criminal record are among the key variables. But prosecutors only give such detailed explanations for their decisions when they are sued, which is rarely, making it easier for everyone to believe the worst in other cases. Judges, by contrast, make their decisions out loud, supported by written opinions that are subject to review by higher courts.

Victoria Toensing, the head of the Justice Department's Criminal Division in the Reagan administration and a key player in the development of the guidelines, says their purpose was truth-in-sentencing, not more power for prosecutors. "Do I want to give [discretion] to a federal judge who has been confirmed by the Senate and supposedly has some experience in the law, or to a 28-year-old prosecutor right out of law school who has no practical experience in his or her life?"[7]

The only reason to deny judges the right to judge is if you believe the pander of right-wing politicians about "liberal" judges who don't like punishment. Yet three-quarters of the federal judiciary were appointed by Republicans, more by President Reagan than anyone else. As for liberals, the Clinton appointees have been ranked by outside evaluators as the ideological equals of President Ford's appointees. Judges continue to be elected in many states, a feat that is almost impossible for anyone described as being a liberal on crime issues. What makes the criticism particularly ironic is that the other group despairing of the quality of the judiciary today is made up of traditional liberals who simply don't get appointed anymore.

The best idea in the federal sentencing guidelines, at least in retrospect, was that judges should be required to state reasons when they imposed sentence, and that sentences should be appealable. Requiring reasons, following precedent, allowing the possibility of reversal by a higher court or by statute—these are the tools of common law. The racial disparities that liberals decried, with reason, might have been addressed not by taking all discretion away from judges but by requiring them to support their decisions with opinions, just like rulings on legal issues, and allowing both sides to appeal. That is how you develop a common law of sentencing. Politics done in the open, subject to constraints, with the legitimacy of law—not the decision of the crowd but the rule of law.

Willie Horton and Richard Alan Davis are easy cases. You don't need long opinions to explain the factors being taken into account. Find me a judge who would let a two-time kidnapper walk, and I'll find you a judge who will be reversed that same day. So, too, I would hope, for the pizza thief and the cologne guy, at least in a system that both allowed discretion and corrected abuses of it on appeal.

But most cases aren't easy. Johnny Houston Holman is more typical. He was the first defendant to be sentenced after the California Supreme Court held that judges must be given discretion under the three-strikes law. He lost his family at 35, started using drugs, and ended up in prison. Since then, he's been convicted half a dozen times, mostly drugs and theft, but he had two armed robberies on his record—one 11 years ago, one 17 years ago. He never hurt anyone. He was arrested when he supposedly dropped a rock of crack in front of two police officers.[8] (Some years ago, the U.S. Court of Appeals in Washington, D.C., wrote an opinion expressing outright disbelief at the number of drug users in the city who allegedly dropped their drugs on the ground upon seeing a police officer—thus bringing the search within the plain view exception to the Fourth Amendment exclusionary rule.)

When I first talked to Johnny Houston Holman, he lamented that if only he had gotten help when things first went wrong, his life might have turned out differently. Was it possible, I wondered, that we had spent literally hundreds of thousands of dollars on him, and were about to spend nearly half a million more (he gets free health care, too), and yet had never provided him drug treatment? Could we be this stupid?

No. Of course not. He'd gotten drug treatment. But he was still using drugs. Holman is not Willie Horton or Richard Alan Davis, but he's not the pizza thief, either. He certainly deserves to be punished, though he's not very dangerous. He's older than average, but in other respects he is typical of why three-strikes laws are so inefficient. What do you do with Johnny Houston Holman? Two years? Four years? Six years? Nothing at all? What factors should you take into account? How do you weigh them? Whose case is most "like" his?

We're back to the eye chart again. How much punishment to impose is a political question—a question of priorities and their application. Ideally, the legislature should set priorities, and judges should apply them, and the end product should be "reasonable" sentences that treat like cases alike, however within reason we choose to define "like." A common law of sentencing. The problem isn't that judges aren't up to their part of the task but that politicians and legislatures have generally done such a poor job of theirs.

Who should prisons be for? The answer coming from the current political debate is that they should be for everybody, which doesn't make much economic sense and isn't feasible anyway. There is certainly a political consensus that violent crime should be a priority and that the most dangerous offenders, whose incapacitation most benefits the rest of us, should be locked up for the longest. But most politicians also pay lip service to a false equality between white-collar crime and street crime and to a hard line on all drug offenses that is impossible to enforce.

What differentiates white-collar felons from street criminals is not only race and economics; it is also dangerousness. The argument that the person who steals in the boardroom is as great a threat to society as the one who steals on the street corner ignores the violation of personal autonomy and the threat to individual human life which explains why all Americans, of every race and income group, put violent crime at the top of their priority list. Nor is this real equality in any event; the number of poor minority teenagers we imprison dwarfs the number of Wall Street insiders a thousand fold; if it is somehow wrong to be punishing so many of them, locking up a Michael Milken or two will hardly make it right.

What really clogs the system is not white-collar criminals but petty thieves and drug users like Johnny Holman. The debate about drugs will go nowhere if it remains a choice between waging the war as though defeat were impossible, or surrendering completely and legalizing all drugs. So long as that is how the question is structured, we will continue to turn our criminal courts into drug courts and our prisons into the most expensive and least effective drug treatment centers in the world. Lock up a robber and, one hopes, you'll have the benefit of fewer robberies—although how many fewer is much debated among criminologists. Lock up a drug courier and he'll be replaced overnight. Granted, drug use is not a victimless crime; its youngest victims are permanently harmed before they are even born. But that doesn't explain our self-defeating absolutism on drugs.

Johnny Houston Holman is lucky to be facing only ten years in jail now, instead of the life term that would have been automatic the day before. Ten years is certainly better than life. But why are we as a society about to spend half a million dollars or more on Johnny Houston Holman? What are we getting for that? I'm not being compassionate; I'm being selfish. It is a waste of my money to lock up a nonviolent, aging crack smoker for the next ten years, when there are so many other, better, more pressing demands on our tax dollars. There is a dire and largely unmet need for other, cheaper ways to punish people who are not dangerous.

In the criminal justice world, we have been talking about this for even longer than we've talked about community policing. What is striking, given the dire need, is how little has been accomplished, and how few leaders are willing to seize the issue and run with it. Creative programs pop up here and there, but political considerations stifle the debate. The risks of being perceived as softhearted or of being blamed when the next Willie Horton rapes someone while on his community service job (which will happen) create a shortage of alternatives, which judges can fill only at the margins. In most cases, if there is to be punishment, the only question is still, How long?

There is no magical number that constitutes the "fair" sentence for robbery or burglary. Does the burglar who is punished for five years instead of five months have any right to complain? Not if the reasons given by the judge for his sentence are reasonable. Was he armed? Was it the third arrest in a short time period? Is there reason to believe that he poses a danger? Why wouldn't we want a wise person asking these questions before spending tens of thousands of our dollars? How else can we make sure we're using our scarce resources wisely, to protect ourselves?

First-year associates at large law firms make more money than most state court judges, and nearly as much as federal judges. Partners in large firms and corporate counsel make many times more than judges. I am not lobbying for an increase in judges' pay, but if being a judge is important, there should be rewards other than financial ones to reflect that. Respect. Honor. Dignity. The right to judge.

What makes a good judge? I think we could use a few "liberals" here and there to stir things up; a Mario Cuomo or a Laurence Tribe would make the intellectual debates on the Supreme Court far more interesting; we already have the conservatives lined up to balance them. But mostly what the courts need are men and women like John Paul Stevens, Sandra Day O'Connor, David Souter, Ruth Bader Ginsburg, and Stephen Breyer—people who are smart and fair, who respect the law, and who try to do their politics honestly.

When I taught advanced criminal procedure at Harvard Law School, an upper-level course, I used to invite Justice Breyer, then a guidelines-maven as Senator Kennedy's designee on the Commission and my former boss on the Judiciary Committee, to teach my class on sentencing day. He's a great teacher and a great judge; he was one of the forces behind airline deregulation, which made his role as the great judicial regulator particularly ironic. He would walk in with his two volumes of sentencing guidelines. Students would start throwing out hypotheticals—and he'd turn first to one page in one book and then back to another to spell out this piece and then back to another to shift the range, in a performance that was stunning. Students would line up after class to make sure they weren't going to be required to learn how to do it for the exam. No wonder so many resigning judges cite the guidelines and the drug laws among their reasons for leaving the bench.

In 1996 the Supreme Court began the long-overdue process of eroding the guidelines, by upholding limited judicial discretion to depart from them—in this case, to give shorter sentences to the police officers convicted of violating the civil rights of Rodney King. The decision was followed only a few weeks later by the California Supreme Court's ruling that untied judges' hands in three-strikes cases.

But even if their hands were untied tomorrow, there is only so much judges can do. They need more real choices, not just greater freedom to pick a number. Even more important, punishment for wrongdoing, no matter who imposes it and what it is, is the exception and not the rule in our system. What do we do about the rest of the crime that is out there, that nobody gets punished for? Who will deal with that?

Politicians and police chiefs trip over each other to claim credit when the crime rate goes down. Some of them do deserve enormous credit for their efforts, particularly in the area of community policing. But demographics has been on their side through much of the decade. Crime is a young man's game. Even as the crime rate has decreased in the last five years, the rate of juvenile crime—particularly violent juvenile crime—has been increasing. In 1995 there were fewer young men between the ages of 16 and 29 than at any point in the last thirty years. As of 1996, the numbers began moving in the opposite direction. The Philadelphia cohort studies have established that each generation of predators is more violent than the one that preceded it. The one that will come of age when my kids do will be the largest since my generation of baby boomers, and it will be far more violent. Princeton professor John DiIulio has called them the "super-predators."[9]

As these young people come of age, the aging population of imprisoned three strikers and drug users will be spending their least dangerous years receiving free medical care in prison. Prison facilities will be scarce, regardless of what we spend. Racial disparities could be even worse than now. The fastest growing groups of 16-to-29-year-olds will be blacks and Hispanics, who are at highest risk for criminal careers. That probably means more crime than the 6 percent projections, perhaps substantially more. It also means that the percentage of the prison population that is black—currently nearing 50 percent—may go even higher.

There is much debate about how much more crime there would be today had we not so dramatically expanded our prison capacity in the last decade. But no serious student of criminology, liberal or conservative, suggests that prison cells alone can make us safe. According to the Rand study, California's three-strikes proposal would require $5.5 billion in additional spending every year to implement, representing a 100 to 150 percent increase in the budget for the Corrections Department, to the point that it would total at least 18 percent of the state budget by 2002. And even then, it would only cut crime by 28 percent. That leaves nearly three-quarters of a potentially growing crime rate.[10]

Why does the crime debate ignore most of the crime? It is, in part, a reflection of the flaws of our political system. Prison guards are among the fastest growing group of public employees, for rather obvious reasons, and they function as a strong and organized lobby for prison building across the country. There is no organization of equivalent strength representing crack babies. To the extent liberals have outlined a crime-prevention agenda, it consists almost exclusively of support for the police. The centerpiece of the 1994 Crime Bill was 100,000 more officers. Across the country, Democrats have been spending time in the back seats of police cars to show that they are tough on crime. In the nonminority community, the police remain the most popular actors in the system; they are amenable to Democratic embrace if only because Democrats do tend to spend more on public employees. Most important, of course, more police, properly deployed, can help cut crime.

Adam Walinsky, a former aide to Senator Robert Kennedy, has argued tirelessly in favor of a liberal embrace of police, promoting a Police Corps to provide tuition incentives for future police officers. For many years, the idea, despite its merits, went nowhere; police unions opposed it, fearing nonunion wages at union expense, and prisons took priority. One of the best provisions of the new crime bill is the measure calling for a prototype ROTC-type police corps.

But the focus on police tends to be partial even on its own

terms. Success is measured numerically: how many additional officers? But there is no direct correlation between per capita policing and the crime rate, and there is a great danger that when numbers count for too much, officers will be put on the street who are undertrained and underequipped, endangering not just themselves and their fellow officers but the people they are paid to protect as well. Stories are legion of police officers who are less well armed than the dangerous criminals they regularly confront—criminals who, these days, carry cell phones and beepers in addition to guns, which is more than most police officers have.

Beyond policing, prevention efforts tend to be a subject of political ridicule rather than common sense support. Because the focus of these programs often comes so late—teenagers or beyond—they are easily tagged as 60s-style failed rehabilitation efforts, even when that isn't so. Studies have found that graduation incentives and parent training actually cut crime more cost-effectively than three strikes. But those efforts don't command top priority even among representatives whose districts stand to gain the most. In the 1994 Crime Bill, the Congressional Black Caucus deserted President Clinton on the Crime Bill because of the absence of any provision addressed to race discrimination in the imposition of the death penalty. The President ended up finding the votes he needed among moderate Republicans, who insisted on cutbacks in prevention programs, many of which would have helped black children and teenagers.

The irony is that the public may understand more than the spooked politicians give them credit for. The California Supreme Court's 1996 ruling giving judges discretion in three-strikes cases met with the immediate outspoken condemnation of Governor Pete Wilson, along with almost every other elected official in the state. Seeing the two-inch newspaper headlines day after day and hearing the rhetoric, one might have thought the prison doors were about to swing open to Willie Horton himself. "Potentially dangerous to public safety" was the Governor's characterization of the decision. In fact, the unanimous decision in *People v. Superior Court,* by a court whose members, except for one, were appointed by tough-on-crime Republican governors, requires judges to state reasons for discounting prior strikes, and makes those decisions appealable—points which the politicians rarely mentioned. What was most striking, however, was that neither the screaming headlines nor the screaming politicians succeeded in alarming the public. In a poll taken a month after the decision, more people supported judicial discretion than a legislative override. The same poll also found that the majority of people thought prevention rather than punishment was the key to reducing crime.[11]

Is it possible that the public is smarter than most politicians think, that they may be willing to move beyond Willie Horton, even if most politicians remain wary? In the early 1980s I participated in a series of Executive Sessions on selective incapacitation and community policing at the Kennedy School of Government at Harvard. Led by Professor Mark Moore, the first series built upon pioneering work by the Rand Corporation on extensive self-reported data from criminals in three states. The exciting conclusion of that report was that robbery could be reduced by 15 percent, and the number of robbers incarcerated could be reduced by 5 percent, if sentences were based on a seven-variable test, with enhanced sentences given to the people with the highest scores.

The Rand test consists of seven factors, none terribly surprising: (1) prior conviction for the same type of offense; (2) incarceration for more than 50 percent of the preceding two years; (3) conviction prior to age 16; (4) serving time in a state juvenile facility; (5) use of hard drugs in the preceding two years; (6) use of hard drugs as a juvenile; and (7) being employed less than 50 percent of the preceding two years. If defendants met four or more factors, their sentences would be enhanced; if they met fewer than four factors their sentences would be reduced. What could be wrong with that?[12]

As the token liberal/civil libertarian/sometime defense lawyer in the group, I took it as my job to figure out if anything *was* wrong. What I kept coming back to was the false-positive problem. When the Rand test identifies someone as a high-rate offender, it is wrong as often as it is right. The formula still works to reduce crime and incarcerations because even such a middling level of accuracy is leaps and bounds better than what we produced before or since. But if one objective of the test is to reduce punishment for those who have committed a crime but are not dangerous, what do you say to the defendant who is wrongly viewed as dangerous when he really isn't? What's the answer to all those people whose sentences we enhance because the test yields false positives as often as it yields true positives?

Easy. The answer is tough luck. The answer is that you don't get to drive until you are 16 no matter how grown up you are. As long as they have a rational basis, rules are rules.

And if the false positives are disproportionately black? This is where it always got tricky. You would never allow a rule that said: "We will lock up the black burglars for three times as long as the white burglars"—no matter how accurate race was in predicting dangerousness. Is a sentencing test that asks about past unemployment and juvenile record all that different? If it turns out to correlate with race, should you still use it?

The irony, in retrospect, is to remember what I tried for so long to put forward instead. Three strikes. I had no problem enhancing someone's sentence based on past convictions. That was my preferred solution: by all means, focus on the career criminal, but define his career by convictions. I might have even settled for arrests. The problem, then as now, was that it won't work. Arrests are only very weakly correlated with self-reported criminal activity. And convictions come too late to make a difference.

The challenge in the criminal justice system is always to avoid letting race make it either too easy or too hard to punish. The answer to the black false positive is that we have a right to fight crime. Would we do the same thing if the false positives were white? Cut crime, and save prison space? Absolutely.

But would we wait until then? If 4 out of 10 of our white sons were facing the likelihood that their lives would be ruined, would our solution be simply to make sure there were enough cemeteries to hold them? Or would we try to make sure that every school had graduation incentives and every child a reason to succeed? Would we limit the debate about juvenile crime to the question of how young is too young to try a child as an adult and lock him away forever? That's a question we need to address, but is it the only one?

How do you go about saving a generation of high-risk six-year-olds? How do you help twelve- and thirteen-year-olds who could still be saved? Of course it can't be done just by government. Of course it takes two parents to raise a child; it takes a family. But what about all those kids who don't have a family? A problem for the private sector, perhaps, or the churches? But no one is stopping the private sector or the churches or synagogues from acting right now. A majority of the black children who will turn 15 in the year 2000 were born to single mothers, and 1 in 14 will have been raised with neither parent at home.[13] How do we protect children who have only one parent, or none at all?

Every criminologist, liberal and conservative, is looking at the same numbers and raising the flags of alarm. Dean James Fox from Northeastern University points out that the 14–17-year-old population will increase 23 percent by 2005. Professor DiIulio forecasts 40,000 homicides, with other violent crimes increasing proportionately. "Look, I'm not a bleeding-heart liberal; I am a realist," Florida's Corrections Commissioner says. "But the cure for our crime is not prison beds and juvenile boot camps. We need to do something about juveniles at the school level before they get here."[14]

But the shadow of Willie Horton gets in the way. We invest too little in prevention, for fear of being seen as soft on crime. Our under-investment in prevention, in turn, exposes the system to charges of racism, which are enough to paralyze but not to liberate liberals. It is not the disproportionate impact of punishment that makes the system racist but the disproportionate impact of our failures at prevention—that is what renders our politics suspect. The only way truly to address racism in the criminal justice system is to cut the crime rate among blacks—to try to inoculate the children, even as we punish so many of their fathers and brothers. It is what we would do if it were our white sons facing their future. It is not racist to lock up Willie Horton. But planning prisons for preschoolers is.

FOUR

Honest Lawyers

"There is a vague popular belief that lawyers are necessarily dishonest," Abraham Lincoln wrote in 1850. "If in your own judgment you cannot be an honest lawyer, resolve to be honest without being a lawyer. Choose some other occupation, rather than one in the choosing of which you do, in advance, consent to be a knave."[1]

My father was a lawyer. He saw his job mostly as helping people, and sometimes as protecting them. One part glue, one part fairness. The glue allowed people to buy and sell houses, start businesses, make deals and also break deals, according to a system of law. The fairness allowed the state to deprive a man of his liberty, lock him up, even take his life, but according to the rule of law rather than simply the assertion of power. He founded the legal aid society in the city where he practiced. He never made much money, but he loved his work.

I grew up believing that being a lawyer was an honorable calling, a profession. The scandal known as Watergate affirmed it. Aspiring journalists celebrated Woodward and Bernstein. I celebrated Cox and Richardson; for me, the heroes of Watergate were the lawyers. The lesson was the triumph of the rule of law; the cause for celebration was that in our society, no one is above the law.

Across the country, many lawyers continue to act as professionals, individually respected, doing what they think is right, displaying quiet integrity. But that is certainly not how the public sees lawyers as a group today, nor is it how we see ourselves. Among professionals, lawyers are among the least satisfied, most disappointed, most alcoholic, and increasingly suicidal in the bunch.[2] My research assistant, a first-year law student, returned depressed when I asked her to survey the literature on lawyer satisfaction. At my husband's twenty-fifth college reunion, virtually all the people at the career-changing workshop were lawyers, many of them the bright stars of the class decades before, wondering where they'd gone wrong. We lawyers yearn for our own mythical fifties, when lawyers were good guys, when partners really were partners, and everyone wanted to go to law school.

Among lawyers, those who practice criminal law are still seen as very much a separate and generally secondary group. But that is not how the public sees it. Criminal lawyers, particularly criminal defense lawyers, have become the celebrities and symbols of our profession. The question whether they are professionals serving principle or brains for hire in the business of helping people get away with murder defines the bar as a whole. The fact that the question arises in practice less often than the public thinks does not diminish the importance of addressing it. Like the best hypotheticals, it presents the question of a lawyer's professionalism in the starkest terms.

It is fundamental to the concept of due process that anyone who is charged with a crime that could result in the loss of liberty has a right to a lawyer, even if he can't afford one. The Supreme Court so held in the landmark 1963 case of *Gideon v. Wainwright*. In our system, the state is put to its proof, not only to protect the innocent but also out of respect for the dignity of the individual. When the forces of the state are arrayed against you, no one should have to stand alone. The adversary system is not the most efficient route to the truth; it doesn't pretend to be. The defendant has the right to remain silent, even when he knows the truth; the right to plead not guilty, even if he is guilty; the right to challenge evidence, even if it is reliable and probative. He has the right to counsel, who will tell him not to confess, not to answer the questions, not to help prosecutors make the case against him.

The question is not whether a lawyer should represent a man he believes is guilty but how far he should go in defending him. Is it the lawyer's job to ensure that the state is put to its proof, that the rights of the individual are respected, that the integrity of the system is preserved? Or is her job to do anything she can, inside or outside the courtroom, to get her client off?

Consider, for example, the hypothetical case offered by Stanford Professor William Simon, in arguing against a lawyer's right to lie. The defendants are on trial for receiving stolen property, which they were transporting in the back seat of a borrowed car. The lawyer knows that when they borrowed the car, they were given only a single key, and that it did not open the trunk. Neither the judge nor the jury knows this. Should the lawyer ask rhetorically, "Why would they put the merchandise in the back seat if they knew it was stolen?" with the clear hope and intent of misleading the jury. Is it ethical?[3]

Could Johnny Cochran ever have believed, even for a moment, that Rosa Lopez was telling the truth? Her plainly incredible testimony, so transparent that ultimately it was not even included in the defense case, was nonetheless the product of careful preparation by the defense attorneys. "Johnny" helped her prepare, presumably so she would answer the questions better. What does "better" mean? Can he tell her what not to say?

There is a long tradition of defense lawyers attempting to destroy the credibility of complainants in rape cases by humiliating them on the stand, a tradition that has been slowed but not stopped entirely by the passage of rape shield laws. When I was raped two decades ago, by a man with an ice pick, the first thing the police warned me about was the possibility that I could be humiliated on the stand. Any old boyfriends who bear a grudge? Anything you'd just as soon not hear about in open court? the cop asked me, as I sat in the back seat of the police car. You know what criminal defense lawyers can do to you, he said, kindly, warning me, in case I didn't want to pursue the case. But the man had an ice pick, I said. Professor Harry Subin describes such an incident from his own career as a criminal defense attorney, where he was ready to pounce on the character of a rape victim even though consent was not at issue.[4]

Lawyers can't just leave all the line-drawing to the judge, and push as far and as hard as a judge will allow them to. In many instances, it is the lawyer, not the judge, who has access to the information needed to evaluate just how much deceit is involved. How is the judge supposed to know that a line has been crossed? He doesn't know that the client had no key to the trunk.

Nor is this one of those decisions that is best left to the market, where competition will produce the optimal end. What makes a lawyer a "good" lawyer—and one worth paying a lot of money for, in the eyes of many clients—is his ability to go to the wall, pull rabbits out of hats, get acquittals where no one else could. If you're a criminal defendant, particularly one who, like most, is guilty, an unethical lawyer is precisely the kind of lawyer you may want.

Society obviously has an interest in not tolerating the techniques of a police state, but it also has an interest in ensuring that the state is capable of imposing responsibility for wrongs. It is better that ten guilty men go free than that one innocent man be punished; but it is best of all if the ten guilty are punished while the innocent man goes free. Indeed, the public perception that the state is no longer strong enough or smart enough to punish the guilty is fueling sometimes ill-considered efforts to restrict the protections afforded to all criminal defendants.

Barbara Babcock, seeking to answer the perennial law school question of why a lawyer would choose to represent someone she knows is guilty, invokes what she calls the social worker's reason: defending the accused is defending the downtrodden and the needy.[5] That is usually the case, but ethical questions rarely arise in those circumstances. The right to counsel guaranteed by the Constitution only guarantees the defendant a warm body. The issue for a poor defendant is not whether his lawyer will lie for him, create reasonable doubt where there isn't any, or undermine truth-telling witnesses but, quite literally, whether he'll even get to meet his lawyer for an interview to give his side of the story before they face the state in court.

Criminal defense lawyers like to tell the story about how we help the poor in standing up for the rich. In asserting the rights of those who can pay our fees to do so, we protect the rights of those who, in future cases, wouldn't be able to pay. Occasionally it is true. The late Professor John Kaplan used to cite the example of challenging a prostitute decoy operation on behalf of a wealthy client that resulted in a change in procedure in which all such encounters were tape-recorded. But it doesn't happen that often.

Most of the time, in asserting the rights of rich defendants, we just help them as individuals. I worked for months with Alan Dershowitz looking for errors in the first trial of Claus von Bulow. The one that finally won reversal of his conviction involved the admission into evidence of two pills that had been turned over to the police (legally) by a private investigator, and then were examined by the police without a warrant. I wish I believed that our efforts on von Bulow's behalf increased the protection of privacy for all the citizens of Rhode Island, but I have absolutely no reason to think that is so. More likely, it produced a backlash against Fourth Amendment claims while reenforcing the public's sense that wealth defines justice, as it often does.

I don't believe for a moment that Johnny Houston Holman really dropped a rock of crack cocaine in front of a police officer. The man I talked to was not that stupid. The LAPD could never have got away with that sort of thing in the O. J. Simpson case. Imagine Rhode Island detectives arguing that von Bulow dropped the black bag containing those pills in front of a police officer. In Johnny Houston Holman's case, the incredible fact apparently made no difference at all. He lacked the resources to prove that the cops were lying even if they were, much less the kind of money it would take to buy a defense that would create that impression with blue smoke and mirrors.

A criminal defense lawyer, the Supreme Court has recognized, has a "special mission" to put the state to its proof. Prosecutors are ethically bound to charge only defendants they believe to be guilty. They are constitutionally required to turn over any evidence that might be helpful to the defendant. A defense lawyer's obligations to the truth are far less clear. There is certainly no requirement that he tell the truth when asked how he pleads his client. His job, in some circumstances, is to help the client divert the search for the truth—for starters, by not talking. But a defense lawyer can't hide the murder weapon in his desk drawer. The "special mission" is the question, not the answer.

The Code of Professional Responsibility plainly states that lawyers should not lie in court under any circumstances. The

merous states have taken a step back from the move to place cameras in courtrooms. That's unfortunate, in most respects, not just for the public but also for the system. In most courtrooms, cameras may well improve the way the criminal justice system functions, and promote the rule of law, in the same way that my defense lawyer friends used to urge me to bring my students to observe court on days they were arguing before unfriendly judges. Authoritarian judges behave better when they're being watched. Defense lawyers at least get to make their arguments. The public might even learn something.

But the power to decide which cases can benefit from television and which ones can't ought to reside in the hands of the person who is responsible for running the courtroom—the judge—not a cable television executive. The primary function of a trial is not to educate the public, much less entertain them, but to assign responsibility; doing that fairly is more important than doing it on television. It is precisely in the high-profile cases with celebrity attorneys and tabloid headlines that the dangers of lawyers, witnesses, and even jurors playing for the cameras are greatest. None of these dangers is beyond the control of a strong judge. But Judge Ito, it bears remembering, was considered one of Los Angeles's best judges when he took over the Simpson case; he was, and will be, a good judge. Few things one learns in law school or in law practice can quite prepare you for what it is like when the national spotlight shines so brightly. Judge Ito made his share of mistakes. He would have made fewer, I think, had there been no cameras.

The same concerns do not apply in courts of appeals. There is no jury; there are no witnesses; there are strict time limits and rules of procedure governing the lawyers. Are we really worried that judges will ask too many questions, be too smart, if the cameras were turned on? It is absurd that we have five hundred cable channels but we do not have television cameras in the Supreme Court of the United States so that people could exult in the rule of law at its best. It is a lost opportunity to see some of the most able advocates in the country, as well as many ordinary country lawyers, engaged in an exercise of rational argument that simply doesn't exist in very many places anymore.

In a Supreme Court argument, the lawyer has no more than thirty minutes, and sometimes less, to try to convince five of the nine; she has to field questions, figure out what's bothering which Justice, try to respond to it, not get sidetracked unless she should get sidetracked to get a vote, not concede anything important, but not avoid a concession that would win a vote she needs, all the while trying to get her own best arguments in and put the other side on the defensive. Some people are brilliant at this timed combination of chess and rhetoric. It is exhilarating to watch Larry Tribe in action, to know what to look for and see how he deals with it, to watch Kathleen Sullivan take a hostile question and turn it around, to see Alan Dershowitz disarm a bench that is prepared for battle.

But the Supreme Court is also a place where a good many regular lawyers come for a day. Getting the Supreme Court to take your case, unless you are the Solicitor General's office (which represents the United States), is like winning—or losing—the legal lottery. Almost no one gives up the chance of an argument before the Supreme Court. They are very nervous, but some of them rise to it magnificently. Mr. Smith comes to Washington on a regular basis in the Supreme Court.

Depending on the case, you would also see the real people whose lives are ultimately being argued about—the kid who didn't want to say the prayer in school, the family that faced housing discrimination. Lorraine Hansberry wrote movingly in *A Raisin in the Sun* about what it was like to grow up in a house in a restricted neighborhood where she and her family had moved in order to be the plaintiffs who had standing to challenge enforced segregation.[8] When I was a law clerk, I always used to watch the faces of the real people.

Justice Stevens likes to tell stories about how he introduces himself as John Stevens, even to lawyers, and no one knows who he is. He doesn't care; what he likes is to surprise folks with his tennis game. I care. Last year, he celebrated his twentieth anniversary on the Court. I think his opinions are far more deserving of attention than what passes as "legal news," the latest stupid lawsuit filed by a publicity-seeking lawyer of whatever ideological bent you like least.

The world of modern communications is defining not only our profession but also our enterprise, while the rules we apply internally date from another era, when lawyers could maintain their integrity and independence by restricting access to the temple. It doesn't work that way anymore. By restricting access we ensure that only the worst will be seen, and that it will come to define us all. Harold Baer, the judge so harshly criticized by President Clinton for his ruling in the cocaine case, turned out be a former federal prosecutor, not a civil libertarian run amok. He had been a member of the Mellon Commission, which investigated police corruption in New York. He may well have been right about the police lying in the case, given that only one officer testified and the other who was present refused to corroborate his account. If Judge Baer had made his charges on *Larry King Live,* instead of ordering a drug courier freed, their impact would have been entirely different. Maybe he should have. At least we need to consider it.

But our problem goes beyond public relations, as do most politicians', when they are languishing in the polls. The business of law has changed dramatically, increasing the competitive pressures that lawyers face. Being a lawyer was never a sure ticket to affluence; most lawyers are lucky if they make as

▼

much as plumbers, and even the most successful earn substantially less than their clients. But there was a certain civility and gentility to the practice of law that contributed to the sense of principled engagement. Ten years ago, I worked for a very prestigious Los Angeles law firm that prided itself on the fact that no partner had ever left to practice with another firm. That was not so uncommon; I met many lawyers in those days, including most of the stars of the profession, who had spent their entire careers at one firm.

But then, thanks to Steve Brill and the *American Lawyer,* everyone started learning about how much everyone else was making, and the out-of-town firms came calling, and the pressure increased to reward the rainmakers by working associates longer hours. Law became an increasingly competitive business; in the next five years, half the partners left my firm to practice at other firms. There is no turning back the clock on many of the external forces that have changed the practice of law. The question lawyers, like doctors and journalists, face is what remains of professionalism in a competitive climate.

It is no longer about what we will do to win but what we won't do. Are we simply the legal tools of those who employ us, the clever translators of their desires, serving no goals but theirs? Win the suit. Get away with murder. Win sympathy for our side on TV. Does our work have no meaning of its own? No wonder we're depressed. Did anyone go to law school to end up this way?

In many respects, our understanding of lawyering is remarkable for how little it has changed. Go back twenty years in a biology class, and they were teaching a different language. Yet I teach the same cases I read as a student. Law professors still quote from decisions made hundreds of years ago, invoking them, distinguishing them, still part of the tapestry. It is not that first principles haven't changed. They have, in fundamental respects. Equality means something totally different today than it did a century ago. But legal argument then was very similar to what legal argument is now; the analytical exercise that is a legal education taught you how to do the same thing. Read the cases, state the rule, state the counter-rule or the distinctions or the political flip-flop, or whatever you choose to call it. Argue how two cases are the same. Argue how they are different. Slice the baloney, the thinner the better; see all the sides, the possibility of things being alike and not alike, and all the reasons why and why not.

What has shifted dramatically over the years is how we view this exercise of doing law. At the beginning of the century, baloney slicing was considered science. Results were thought to be compelled, not chosen, the product of finer and more insightful line drawing. That myth was exposed by the legal realists, who laid bare the realities of judicial value choices in the making of law. Then came the legal-process generation, the postrealist traditionalists, the people who found in the processes of decision making—respect for precedent, the requirement of reasoned elaboration, the baloney-slicing of it all—the limits on politics that allow us to call what we do law.

The critical legal studies movement saw legal-process people as protectors of the status quo. The crits, based at Harvard where I studied and taught, mocked them as baloney-slicers engaged in a fraudulent exercise of self-delusion. The crits saw their mission as stripping bare the capitalistic, sexist, racist underpinning of the law as a power tool, beginning with the law school itself. While the fights raged at Harvard, the economists were taking over everywhere else, arguing that economic efficiency should tell you how to slice the baloney, an approach that has never taken hold as firmly in criminal law as it has on the civil side.

All of these movements are, in a sense, an effort to answer

the same question: To what end? It's not just a question of what judges do. It is also an effort to answer the question of what lawyers are doing with our legal skills. If now we know how to approach a problem, break it into ever smaller pieces, turn it into questions, compare and contrast the pieces, see how the argument works, see where it misses a point, what do we do with that ability? To what end?

To make money, to be sure. And to serve our clients, no question. But is there anything else? Anything more? What are lawyers, if not merely hired guns? How do we decide how far to go in representing a client, what tactic to use in undermining a witness, how far to push a client's advantage, what counts as a "lie"? Part of the answer is what you can get away with, what Justice Holmes's famous "bad man" would do. In defining the difference between law and morality, Justice Holmes refers to the perspective of the bad man, concerned not with what is right and wrong but with what he can be punished for. If you want to understand the criminal law, Justice Holmes pointed out, you look at it from the perspective of the bad man, for whom it sets the boundaries.[9]

But that really is just one part. The other part is the standard we apply to ourselves, the question of whether we are acting as priests of the temple or agents of its destruction. Are we furthering the rule of law or undermining it, increasing faith in the rule of law or destroying it? Are we seeing to it that the system works, or doing our best to see that it doesn't? Are we professionals or prostitutes?

Of course it is a political standard, not a scientific test, an invitation to any first-year law student to argue this side and that. "Our job is not to sit in judgment of our clients," lawyers say all the time. True enough—it is not our clients we should be judging but ourselves.

Protecting the rule of law should be the focus of the concerted efforts of lawyers. Lawyers are powerful politically. The

American Trial Lawyers Association enjoys a special place in the hearts of most Democrats, and they wield enormous influence on issues of tort liability. But that power is not used in other fights where the rule of law is most surely equally at stake.

It is criminal that our profession is so weak, our organization and leadership so compromised, our heroes so lacking in credibility, that we as lawyers can do nothing to protect the judiciary from the current round of demonization and politicization that threatens its independence and integrity. It is tragic that a President who obviously understands all the reasons why Presidents shouldn't attack sitting judges feels that he has no choice but to do so. But what is ultimately just as troubling is the fact that the defense of judicial independence offered by the conservative Chief Justice of the United States mattered not at all to the hordes of politicians who preceded and succeeded the President in calling for Judge Baer's head.

How many Americans could recognize the Chief Justice of the United States? How many even know his name? The American Bar Association has become such an easy target that Republicans in the United States Senate have found that there is no political price to be paid for ignoring it altogether, or even scoring points at its expense. It is not so much that the Bar is viewed as liberal by conservatives; it is viewed as representing lawyers—translation, lawyers' economic interests—by almost everyone.

The obligation to pro bono service should encompass both sides in the criminal justice system. Not everyone wants to be a defense lawyer. Fine. Help the prosecution. As the lawyers and law professors lined up to help O. J. Simpson, it was striking to see how quickly the usually dominant prosecutors were outsmarted. Where were all the civic-minded lawyers and law professors who might have helped the rule of law be enforced? The prosecution took offense at my suggestion that they should line up their own dream team, but they were wrong. They did need help. The case was too important to the community to lose because of better lawyering on the other side.

In the last analysis, however, the most important judgments a lawyer makes as a professional are the invisible, individual ones, the ones where the bad man could get away with it, but the good man knows that it is wrong. Sometimes press coverage is the only way to bring attention to a just cause. Sometimes press coverage is a tool to distort and deceive, to do outside the courtroom what would be prohibited on the inside. That is not a line that can be drawn from the outside; it is not a standard that others can enforce.

One criminal defense lawyer I know, a very successful partner in a major firm, told me he had made peace with the fact that he would never get the big cases. He doesn't have a reputation for scorched-earth defense tactics. Rich guys willing to spend every dime to push the state to the wall don't hire him. He is not the baddest "bad man." He obeys the discovery rules, instead of turning them into a game to see what he can get away with. His word means a great deal. He does not believe juries should be political tools, and he would not be comfortable manipulating them to send messages. He would attack police racism only if he had some reason to believe it had affected the way the police treated his client. He prefers never to voice opinions about his clients' guilt or innocence, so as not to have to lie or implicate by silence. He has no desire to be recognized at restaurants or rock concerts. But if, God forbid, your kid got picked up for drugs, you would want this man to represent him. The kid would learn something, without his life being ruined. Ideally, he would help your kid straighten up, not just get off.

There are many lawyers like him. Virtually every criminal defense lawyer I know lives according to ethical rules that they impose on themselves, not because they'd go to jail otherwise but because they take ethics seriously. Most lawyers try to do what is "right" not simply because someone might catch them but because that is the business we are supposed to be in. But you don't hear much about them. They are not the heroes they should be.

Los Angeles Mayor Richard Riordan, who was an extremely successful lawyer and investor before running for mayor, gave the commencement speech at USC Law School's 1995 graduation. He used the occasion to take strong issue with the comments of Alan Dershowitz, who had been much in the news for his attacks on the city. But what earned the Mayor's particular ire was the view Dershowitz had taken that a lawyer, a good lawyer, could not be a mensch.

Can we be men and women of honor and decency, the good people of our communities, and still be tough and smart? Can we stand for the rule of law and accept our responsibility to preserve it? We who are lawyers know how to use our skills to tear people apart. We know how to argue, how to fight, how to disagree. But the greatest need of an increasingly diverse country is not for those whose skill is to divide people but for those who see the common ground while the rest of us are blinded by our differences. That's lawyering, too; the law can be the glue that holds us together.

Epilogue

In December 1996—just weeks before the jury in the second
O. J. Simpson trial delivered its verdict—the *Los Angeles Times*
published a stunning three-part series which established that a
majority of those who commit murder in Los Angeles County
each year do indeed get away with it. Only half of all homicide
investigations lead to arrests, and only 16 percent of the
killings in a four-year period resulted in a murder conviction.

Why are so many people getting away with murder in LA?
There are many reasons, according to the report. As killings move
out of homes and into streets, they are harder to solve. Even
when the police get credible leads, they are so overwhelmed
that the follow-up tends to be sloppy and inadequate, compro-
mising the possibility of a murder conviction. In many cases,
particularly where gangs are involved, witnesses are reluctant
to come forward, and cases regularly fall apart.

Charges of racism abound. Do killings of whites get taken
more seriously than killings of blacks? The data would seem to
suggest so. But is that because the victims are white, or because
their neighbors are more likely to be cooperative, or because
white victims are more likely to be the sort of "innocent" victims the system has always protected best, regardless of race?

And if white deaths are being taken more seriously by the criminal justice system, are black killers getting off easier overall, since most of their victims are black? Two national studies have so found.

In January 1997, as President Clinton delivered his State of the Union address, the second jury delivered its verdict that Simpson was liable for the deaths of Nicole Brown and Ronald Goldman. The final act in this American tragedy was not the jury's verdict, however, but the failure of that verdict to change anyone's mind along the racial divide.

After the criminal verdict of "not guilty," a CNN poll found that 73 percent of all whites and 27 percent of all blacks personally thought O. J. Simpson murdered his former wife and Ronald Goldman. After the civil verdict of liability, 77 percent of all whites and 28 percent of all blacks said they thought he had committed the acts. Statistically speaking, no change. Measures of approval and disapproval of the verdict, sympathy for O. J. Simpson, and approval of the award of compensatory damages tracked on racial lines as well.

The most common explanation of the racial divide was that it reflected the very different experiences that blacks have with police. But that's only half the story. The experience many blacks have with police racism never applied to O. J. Simpson, as virtually everyone acknowledges. Unlike almost every other black man in LA, he did not need to worry about being mistaken for a thug.

"Do you really believe O. J. Simpson didn't do it?" I asked a black radio caller, who said that he had been "rooting" for O. J. all along. "That isn't the point," he replied. Saying that O. J. Simpson is innocent is as much an expression of what side you're on as it is of who you think did it. It is a measure of political allegiance and political distrust, not a conclusion of fact.

I always liked my Frank Capra ending to the O. J. story: the jurors would find him guilty based on the evidence, and then march en masse to the office of the Chief of Police and Mayor and demand changes or else. Think how much might have been accomplished. They could have united the community. They could have been a voice for change.

"Dream on, Susan," one of my black students tells me. How could you possibly expect jurors who had never done politics in their lives to understand that there might be a better way to do it? Politics is something you need to learn to do—something you have to practice—to do well.

▼   ▼   ▼

In most law school exams, the test is to see how many different crimes or causes of action you can find in a single set of facts. In criminal law, there's almost always a killing, and the best student can argue it as murder, manslaughter, felony murder, reckless homicide, depraved heart, involuntary manslaughter, battery, or even no crime at all. The more possibilities you think of, the better you do. In real life, judgment is all about narrowing the possibilities. The jury that convicted Louise Woodward was right, as far as it got to go. People who cause death by their intentional acts should not get away with it; technically, they may be convicted of murder. But such killings are usually considered manslaughter at most, not murder; people who kill unintentionally are guilty, but less guilty.

Louise Woodward was overcharged, either to give leverage to the prosecutors (which is common) or to avoid charges that the prosecutor was "soft" in a highly publicized case (which is becoming increasingly common). Her lawyers had the smarts and skill to call the prosecutors' bluff, and they did. The lawyers poked enough holes in the prosecution's case that most close observers were convinced that their decision to limit the jury instructions to an up or down vote on murder was a brilliant move. As it turned out, it wasn't so brilliant. But trials aren't chess games, and they shouldn't be. Judge Zobel rightly refused to second-guess the strategic judgment, or to force Woodward to bear its consequences. The defendant's rights were respected, but the jury was cheated of its chance to judge.

Days after Woodward was convicted, a Missouri judge's decision to sentence to probation a 21-year-old father who admitted shaking his son to death in frustration because of the boy's crying provoked public outrage and made newspapers across the country. A week earlier, it would not have been noted. Until O. J. Simpson, it was routine for men to get away with murdering unfaithful wives, or at least to serve no more than five years for it. Today, it is common to hear defense lawyers claim that such men are singled out for especially harsh treatment. A new political accommodation is being made. Louise Woodward did not get away with murder. She stands convicted of manslaughter. She served nine months in prison. It is not as long a sentence as many of us would favor, but it is longer than most parents have served in the past. The sand is shifting in the political winds.

▼　　▼　　▼

How many of you voted in the last election, I ask my undergraduate students? Half the hands go up. We are raising a generation of civic illiterates—a generation of students who would not dream of graduating college without computer skills but who look blankly at me when I ask the names of their congressmen.

In 1962, in *Baker v. Carr,* the United States Supreme Court held for the first time that every person's vote in this country must count for the same: one man, one vote. Chief Justice Earl Warren, the former California Governor and the last great politician on the Court, once said that if *Baker v. Carr* had been decided earlier, the Court would never have been forced to decide *Brown v. Board of Education*. A representative political system would not have segregated schoolchildren based on race. Chief Justice Warren believed in politics.

So do I. But politics isn't just the last resort when all our theories of jurisprudence have failed. To believe in the rule of law in a democracy, as I do, is to believe in a way of doing politics built on faith in one another's good intentions, however misinformed, naive, or even stupid we may sometimes be. Politics is the way we work out how to live together. At its best it involves compromise, reciprocity, compassion. At its worst it dissolves into name-calling, cynicism, and distrust. Doing politics, in one form or another, is the inevitable price we pay to live in a society. *How* we do it, both inside and outside the criminal justice system, will define what kind of society ours will be.

Top Ten Sympathy Defenses

Over the years, my students and I have been keeping a list of cases in which "sympathy defenses" are raised. Our effort leaves no doubt that while most defendants do *not* get away with murder by appeals to sympathy, more of them try than one might expect, and they are successful often enough to contribute to the public's doubts about the system as a whole. Herewith, an alphabetical top ten list.

1. Adopted Child Syndrome

Usually used to support an insanity plea, the defense asserts that the trauma of adoption, a fear of abandonment, and feelings of powerlessness and rejection may produce a psychotic, insane rage which causes sufferers to strike out, often at his or her adoptive parents.

- Used in 1986 by Patrick DeGelleke, 15, who set his parents' bedroom on fire with them inside. Both died. DeGelleke was found guilty of second-degree murder and arson. DeGelleke was sentenced to four concurrent sentences of 7 years to life plus a concurrent arson sentence.

- Used in 1988 by Patrick Campbell, 20, in the hatchet and sledgehammer slaying of his adoptive parents. Campbell was sentenced to 45 years in prison.

- Used in 1993 by Matthew Heikkila, 20, who killed his adoptive parents with bullets labeled Mom and Dad. He was found guilty of murder but was spared the death penalty. Heikkila was sentenced to 60 years in prison.

The adopted child syndrome defense received attention from the trial of serial killer Joel Rifkin, who tried to use the defense to support an insanity plea.

2. Battered Child Syndrome

This defense is usually used to support a self-defense claim; the defense contends that because of years of abuse a battered child may have a reasonable fear of imminent and severe abuse even if that threat would be imperceptible to an outsider, because the child is attuned to the stages of violence of the attacker. Thus, the battered child's syndrome is used to explain why a child's actions may be reasonable even though not fitting into the traditional model of self-defense.

▶ Used by Erik and Lyle Menendez to validate a self-defense claim in the killing of their mother and father. After an initial mistrial, a second jury found them guilty of murder in the first degree.

▶ Used by John Bradshaw Jr., 23, to support his self-defense claim in the killing of his father. Bradshaw lay in wait and shot his father in the head; his father had threatened him earlier in the day. Bradshaw, tried for murder, was convicted of the reduced charge of voluntary manslaughter.

▶ Herman and Druie Dutton, 15 and 12, pleaded no contest to manslaughter in the shooting death of their sleeping father, who reportedly beat them and sexually abused their sister. The boys received an outpouring of public support and won't be punished or have criminal records if they stay out of trouble for 31 months, when Herman turns 18.

3. Battered Woman/Husband Syndrome

The BWS is often used with a self-defense plea when women kill their abusive partners. Expert testimony on the BWS is used to explain why a woman would stay with an abusive mate and the effect of repeated assaults and threats on her ability to cope effectively with her situation. Testimony regarding the BWS can demonstrate why a battered woman may perceive a threat differently than other victims or why a battered woman doesn't retreat from a violent situation.

- In 1994 Lorena Bobbitt asserted that she cut off her sleeping husband's penis after he had beaten and raped her earlier that night. She was found not guilty by reason of insanity.

- In a similar case, Aurelia Macias was acquitted of mayhem and assault with a deadly weapon after she cut off her husband's testicles with a scissors. Macias claimed she acted only in self-defense, after years of physical abuse; prosecutors in the case contended that she attacked her husband because he was flirting with another woman at a party. The prosecutor has decided that Macias should be retried on a battery charge on which the jury had deadlocked, but Macias has reconciled with her husband, who did not want to press charges.

- The BWS defense was allowed in the 1994 murder-for-hire trial of Mary Stiles. Stiles hired a man to kill her wheelchair-bound husband, sideshow performer Grady Stiles Jr. aka Lobster boy. Stiles alleged that her husband rammed into her and her son with his wheelchair, butted them with his head, and hit them with his clawlike arms. Stiles was convicted on a lesser charge of manslaughter and sentenced to 12 years in prison.

The battered husband's syndrome is similar to the battered woman's syndrome, but often the abuse is more psychological than physical and may include badgering, nagging, and belittling.

- Used, along with a cultural defense, by Moosa Hanoukai in 1994. Hanoukai killed his wife after years of being browbeaten, "psychologically emasculated," called "stupid" and "idiot" and made to sleep on the floor. Hanoukai was convicted of a lesser charge of voluntary manslaughter and sentenced to 11 years in prison.

► In 1987 Stanley Tvarian strangled his wife Joan after what he claims were years of physical, verbal, and emotional abuse. Their daughter agreed that her mother hit her husband many times and would "curse him for not being enough of a man." Tvarian pleaded guilty to manslaughter and was sentenced to a maximum five-year prison term; he would be eligible for work release in two years.

► In 1988 James Holloman was found guilty of the reduced charges of voluntary manslaughter and reckless endangerment in the beating death of his wife; prosecutors had sought a first-degree murder conviction. Defense attorneys portrayed 135-pound Holloman as a victim of spousal abuse who feared his 300-pound wife. Sentencing information was not available.

4. Cultural Defenses

A cultural defense (or as some prefer, cultural evidence) may be asserted when a member of a minority culture contends that he or she violated a criminal law because they were following the customs or traditions of his or her own culture.

► The defense was raised when a Japanese-American woman, Fumiko Kimura, attempted to commit parent-child suicide when she learned of her husband's affair. Her children died, but she survived. According to her attorney, in traditional Japanese culture the ritual is an accepted means for a woman to rid herself of the shame accompanying infidelity. Kimura was allowed to plead guilty to voluntary manslaughter and was given probation.

► Kong Moua, a Hmong tribesman living in California, kidnapped a woman from a local college. Moua called it *zij poj niam,* or "marriage by capture," an accepted form of matrimony in his culture; his victim, also a Hmong, called it kidnapping and rape. Moua was able to plead to a lesser charge of false imprisonment after introducing literature about Hmong customs. He was sentenced to 120 days in jail and a $1000 fine.

▸ The defense (as well as an abused husband defense) was used by Iranian immigrant Moosa Hanoukai, who killed his wife after years of her challenging his manhood, violating the norms of their Iranian Jewish culture. He was prevented from getting a divorce because of their cultural beliefs. He was convicted of voluntary manslaughter and sentenced to 11 years in prison.

5. Husbands Who Kill

▸ In 1988 Judge Carol Irons was shot to death in her chambers by her estranged husband, Clarence Donald Ratliff, an off-duty police officer, who then fired at other officers before surrendering. Ratliff was jealous about Irons's supposed infidelities with other men. Jurors in the case were not allowed to hear about assaults that Ratliff had made on his first wife. Tried for murder, Ratliff was convicted of a lesser charge of voluntary manslaughter in the death of Irons and assault with intent to commit murder in the shots fired at police officers, none of which were hit. One juror said "everybody felt he was provoked by his wife to do this. First of all she went out with other men. Then he was having trouble sexually, and I imagine she rubbed that in to him . . . All of that provoked him into doing it." Public protest ensued when it was discovered that manslaughter carries only a maximum penalty of 15 years, while the attempted murder of officers carries a possible life prison sentence. Ratliff's defense attorney stated, "It was obvious the jury felt stronger about shooting the police officers than shooting his wife." Ratliff was sentenced to 10 to 15 years for the slaying of Irons, and two life terms for firing at the officers. Ratliff could be considered for parole in 10 years.

▼

▸ In 1988 Terrence Ruza, previously convicted of killing his wife, was charged with the murder of his girlfriend, whose body was found stuffed inside a shipping barrel, shot several times in the head. Ruza had served 2 years of a 4-year sentence for the manslaughter conviction in the slaying of his wife; he had been charged with first-degree murder in that case, but testimony that his wife may have been having an extramarital affair persuaded the jury to convict him of the lesser charge. Ruza was convicted of second-degree murder and faced a maximum sentence of 22 years to life in prison for the murder of his girlfriend.

▸ In August 1994 Jimmy Jones received a harsher sentence for an unsuccessful attempt to blow up his wife, Karen, than he did for stabbing her to death a few weeks later. Jones was convicted of a lesser charge of voluntary manslaughter in the stabbing death of his wife; he argued that she was angry about an affair that he was having and he was afraid she might be carrying a gun. For the homicide, Jones was sentenced to 10 to 25 years and will be eligible for parole in 5 years. Jones was later sentenced in federal court to 10 years in prison (with no parole) for a conviction of manufacturing and possessing a bomb. Jones had placed model rocket engines in the gas tank of his wife's car and wired them to the light on the rear license plate; the rockets were supposed to have detonated when Karen turned on the car's lights. The U.S. District judge made the federal sentence run at the same time as the state court sentence because she found that both crimes were part of a continued effort to kill Karen Jones.

▸ In 1989 Dong Lu Chen was sentenced to only 5 years' probation for the homicide of his wife, who he suspected of having an affair. Chen smashed his wife Gian Wan's head eight times with a hammer. Chen was convicted of a reduced charge of manslaughter. The sentencing judge noted that Chen's "cultural background . . . made him more susceptible to cracking under the circumstances." (This case could also be considered a cultural defense.)

▸ In February 1994 Carl Berk argued that his wife's adultery led him to kill her and her lover when he walked in on them in bed together. The defense painted a portrait of Mrs. Berk as a manipulative adulteress with a taste for younger men and life in the fast lane. Berk was found guilty of second-degree murder in the killing of his wife and manslaughter in the death of her lover. He was sentenced to 29 years to life.

6. Mob Mentality/Riot Syndrome Defense

The defense asserts a "group contagion" theory—that a mob scene can cause an individual to act impulsively in a way that he or she ordinarily would not, because of the frenzy going on around him or her.

▸ The defense was used in the 1993 trial of Damian Williams and Henry Watson for their riot-related assaults. Williams was found not guilty of attempted murder and aggravated mayhem and found guilty only of simple mayhem against Reginald Denny and four counts of misdemeanor assault involving other victims. Henry Watson was convicted only of misdemeanor assault.

7. Mothers Who Kill

Some mothers may kill in reaction to a real or imagined threat to their children. This is sometimes called the Mother-Lion Defense.

▸ On April 2, 1993, Ellie Nesler walked into a California courtroom and shot to death Daniel Driver, who was there for a preliminary hearing. Driver had been accused of molesting five boys, including Nesler's son. A jury found her guilty of voluntary manslaughter, the lowest charge against her. She has since been released on parole.

▸ In 1992 Tina Marie Werly arranged for the shotgun killing of her one-time boyfriend, Gregory Kittle, who she was convinced was molesting their three-year-old daughter. Her attorney asserted that Werly felt powerless when authorities failed to prosecute Kittle on molestation charges and a judge ordered joint custody of the child; the molestation charges were never proved. Werly, charged with first-degree murder, was convicted of a lesser charge of voluntary manslaughter. Werly received a 12-year sentence.

Postpartum psychosis is a severe emotional imbalance occurring after pregnancy in a small percentage of women. These new mothers often have difficulty coping with the care of the infant, and may appear confused, fatigued, and have delirium, hallucinations, and insomnia. The women often have excessive concern about the baby's health, guilt about lack of love, and delusions about the baby being deformed or dead. The defense is sometimes used by women who kill their infants, and has been quite successful.

- In 1987, Sheryl Massip threw her six-week-old son into the path of a car, hit him over the head with a tool, and then backed over him in the family station wagon. She testified about her postpartum disorders at trial. She was convicted of second-degree murder but the trial court reduced the conviction to voluntary manslaughter and found her not guilty by reason of insanity.

- In 1985 Ann Green tried to kill her third child by holding a pillow over its face. She then became aware of what she was doing and sought help. She later admitted to suffocating her first two children in 1980 and 1982. Green was acquitted by reason of insanity of two counts of second-degree murder and one count of attempted murder and ordered to undergo treatment.

8. Posttraumatic Stress Disorder (War-related)

Often used with an insanity plea, war-related PTSD asserts that veterans of wars often suffer from flashbacks, paranoia, depression, rage, and episodes in which the sufferer acts without control while reliving a traumatic experience. Posttraumatic Stress Disorder has been included in the APA's *Diagnostic and Statistical Manual* since 1980.

- ▶ In 1981 Charles Heads was found not guilty by reason of insanity in the shooting death of his brother-in-law. Heads asserted that he believed that he was back in Vietnam combat when the killing occurred.

- ▶ In 1980 Michael Tindall was acquitted on a drug smuggling charge by a jury who accepted his argument that his experiences in Vietnam made him seek out the thrills and excitement he had felt in combat even if they were outside the law.

- ▶ In 1982 Jearl Wood was found not guilty by reason of insanity of the charges of attempted murder, aggravated battery, and armed violence stemming from the shooting of his plant foreman. His defense attorneys argued that Wood was suffering from a delayed reaction to combat stress he had experienced in Vietnam.

- ▶ In 1991 sailor Walter Thomas used PTSD in his trial for murdering a 21-year-old acquaintance and her 3-year-old daughter. Thomas claimed that he had been driven insane by the 1987 Iraq attack that killed 37 of his shipmates. Thomas was convicted of both murders and given two consecutive life sentences.

- ▶ In 1993 Carl Chichester was convicted of capital murder and armed robbery and sentenced to life. Chichester asserted that he suffered from PTSD because he was a Marine stationed in Beirut during the bombing of the Marine barracks there; prosecutors showed that Chichester did not even join the Marines until four months after the incident.

9. Urban Survival Syndrome

This defense asserts that people living in urban areas can suffer from a type of posttraumatic stress syndrome—victims of violent surroundings, senseless killings, intense peer pressure, and low self-esteem. We can also apply such a defense to others who react violently after continuous exposure to violent surroundings, such as police and crime "victims" turned vigilantes like Bernhard Goetz.

- In 1994 the defense was successful in forcing a mistrial (11 to 1 to convict) in the case of 18-year-old Damion Osby, tried for shooting to death two men. The defense contended that Osby had a heightened fear of the two men because they were all young, black males living in a high-crime neighborhood.

- A variant of urban survival has been used as a defense for police crimes; the stress officers face on the job has been used to explain unduly aggressive police behavior. In a survey conducted by city attorney James Hahn's office in 1991, 53.6 percent of LAPD officers cited fear of personal injury as the reason for police violence.

10. Vigilantes

- In October 1994, Mitchell Gohman chased and killed a man suspected of shoplifting a 12-pack of beer from a convenience store. It is unclear how the suspect died, but Gohman had put him in a head lock. No charges were filed against Gohman.

- In 1990 Victor Lopez, 18, hunted down and stabbed to death a man he believed had mugged and molested his mother earlier in the day. Lopez was charged with first-degree manslaughter, but a grand jury failed to indict him on these charges.

- In 1992 Rodney Peairs was acquitted of manslaughter in the shooting death of a 16-year-old Japanese exchange student, Yoshihiro Hattori. Hattori approached Peairs's home looking for a Halloween party and didn't understand when Peairs ordered him to freeze. Peairs shot him with a .44 caliber revolver, hitting him once in the chest. In September of 1994 the parents of Hattori won a $653,000 judgment against Peairs for the death of their child.

▸ In 1987 Raymond Wisecarver was convicted of the lesser charge of manslaughter in the shooting death of Edward Shreckengaust, a man suspected of raping his 15-year-old stepdaughter. Wisecarver's stepdaughter had reported to police that Shreckengaust had raped her in his apartment. Detectives had declined to arrest Shreckengaust pending further investigation; they had some doubts about the girl's allegations because she at first failed to report that she and Shreckengaust had used cocaine during the evening of the alleged assault. After learning that Shreckengaust had not been arrested, Wisecarver went to his house posing as a magazine salesman. Wisecarver was sentenced to 8 years in prison, making him eligible for parole in 3 years.

▸ In 1990 Vahag Babayan was acquitted of second-degree murder and manslaughter in the shooting death of two men who had just robbed his jewelry store. Babayan chased after the robbers, shooting repeatedly at them as they sat inside their getaway car, even after one suspect begged him to stop.

▸ In 1984 Gary Plauche shot and killed Jeffrey Doucet, a karate instructor that he suspected had kidnapped and sexually assaulted his 11-year-old son. Doucet was killed after being led off an airplane by arresting deputies who were returning him from California, where he had taken Plauche's son. The event was recorded live by television cameras. Plauche pleaded no contest to a charge of manslaughter; he received a 7-year suspended sentence, with five years probation.

▸ In 1986 in Pacoima, California, David Mota was captured and beaten to death with fence posts by an outraged crowd after he shot and killed a teenager and injured three other men at a party. Prosecutors decided not to file charges against the mob, because they could not prove that the killing was not justifiable as self-defense.

- In 1988 Raymondo Caraballo was beaten to death by an angry crowd in Spanish Harlem who suspected him of stealing $20 from a neighborhood bakery. Four men were charged in the beating death with first- and second-degree murder. Charges were dropped because of insufficient evidence against all suspects except for Jesus Negron. Negron later pleaded guilty to second-degree manslaughter in exchange for a sentence of from 3 to 6 years in prison.

- In 1988 Angelo Parisi and Perry Kent were acquitted of arson in the burning of a house in their neighborhood that was suspected of being used by drug dealers, even though the men admitted starting the fires. The men testified that drug dealers had turned their neighborhood into a place of fear and that they set fire to the house after police failed to investigate the complaints they had filed. Their attorneys argued that their clients had acted under duress and in self-defense.

Notes

Prologue

1. A 1997 poll by the Washington, D.C.-based Joint Center for Political and Economic Studies found that 81 percent of blacks and 83 percent of Hispanics believe that police are far more likely to harass and discriminate against blacks than whites; 56 percent of whites agreed. A 1997 *New York Times* poll found that 82 percent of black New Yorkers and 71 percent of Hispanic New Yorkers believe police do not treat whites and blacks with equal fairness. See Julia Vitullo-Martin, "Fairness, Justice Not Simply Black and White," *Chicago Tribune*, November 13, 1997. In a CNN-USA Today poll, 33 percent of blacks—compared with 70 percent of whites—believed that the police generally testify truthfully. See Maria Puente, "Poll: Blacks' Confidence in Police Plummets," *USA Today*, March 21, 1995. See generally R. Kennedy, *Race, Crime and the Law* (Pantheon, 1997).

1. Politics and the Reasonable Man

1. American Law Institute, *Model Penal Code and Commentaries*, The American Law Institute (1980–1985).
2. Oliver Wendell Holmes Jr., *The Common Law* (Little, Brown, 1881).
3. The Model Penal Code defines manslaughter to include "homicide which would otherwise be murder . . . committed under the

11. Maura Dolan, "Judging the Jury System: Is Justice Being Served?" *Los Angeles Times*, September 27, 1994, p. A1.

12. Nancy M. Marder, "Beyond Gender: Peremptory Challenges and the Roles of the Jury," 73 *Texas Law Review* 1041 (1995).

3. The Long Shadow of Willie Horton

1. Elizabeth Alexander, "Symposium on Federal Sentencing, the New Turn of the Screw," 66 *Southern California Law Review* 209 (1992), reports that the United States has the highest incarceration rate in the industrialized world, a lead that increases each year without a corresponding decrease in crime; a 1/3 decrease in crime would require a 450 percent increase in the incarceration of offenders. Anne Morrison Piehl and John J. DiIulio Jr., *Does Prison Pay Revisited* (Brookings Institute, 1995), reconfirm earlier findings that prison does pay but with a caveat, the public could benefit from removing 10–25 percent of inmates from custody. Drug offender incapacitation is found to have a social value of zero, as incarcerated offenders are readily replaced by new dealers.

2. David B. Kopel, *Prison Blues: How America's Foolish Sentencing Policies Endanger Public Safety* (Cato Institute, 1994); Study by the Center on Juvenile and Criminal Justice, San Francisco, California, March 4, 1996; Marc Mauer, "Intended and Unintended Consequences: Racial Disparities in Imprisonment," Sentencing Project, 1997.

3. Marvin Wolfgang et al., *Delinquency in a Birth Cohort* (University of Chicago Press, 1972), is the original source of the 6 percent rule.

4. RAND Corporation, *Three Strikes Would Cut Crime But High Costs Make Full Effects Unlikely; Other Sentencing Options Could Achieve Crime Reductions at Less Cost* (RAND, 1994).

5. *Cato Press Release*, May 17, 1994, p. 93. Lou Cannon, "Tough Talk, Longer Prison Sentences Won't Save Kids," *Seattle Post-Intelligencer*, December 13, 1993, p. A13.

6. "The Crime Funnel," *New York Times Magazine*, June 12, 1994. The 35 million crimes committed each year pour in at the top of the funnel—crimes ranging from shoplifting and auto theft to

rapes and murders. Millions of these crimes go unpunished because the victims never report them; year after year the number of crimes people say they experience far exceeds the number of reported crimes. That is the first narrowing of the funnel. The next comes at the level of apprehension. The police make arrests in only 21 percent of the 15 million most serious crimes each year; as a result 3.5 million criminals are turned over to the court for prosecution. The funnel narrows even further at the courthouse level. Many cases are dismissed for lack of evidence, or because witnesses disappear or refuse to cooperate. So of the 3.5 million criminals arrested, 81 percent are actually prosecuted; of those, 59 percent are convicted. In the end, of the 1.9 million convicts, only 500,000 are sent behind bars—merely a sprinkle from the funnel's stem compared with the flood of 35 million at its mouth.

7. Harvey Berkman, "Court to Take on Sentencing Rules: A 10-year-old Dispute between Prosecutors, Judges over Federal Guidelines Goes to the High Court," 18 *National Law Journal* 20 (1996).

8. Alan Abrahamson, "Quick Change Hours after High Court's '3 Strikes' Decision," *Los Angeles Times*, June 22, 1996, p. A18.

9. John J. DiIulio Jr., "Moral Poverty: The Coming of the Super-Predators Should Scare Us into Wanting to Get to the Root Causes of Crime a Lot Faster," *Chicago Tribune*, December 15, 1995.

10. RAND Corporation, *Three Strikes Would Cut Crime but High Costs Make Full Effects Unlikely* (RAND, 1994).

11. A poll of the Los Angeles Media Market asked participants questions regarding youths and crime. Among respondents, 19 percent said that it is too late to help a young person involved with crime by the age of 18, 82 percent felt we should invest in crime prevention rather than building prisons, and 57 percent would be willing to transfer money from the prison budget to community youth violence prevention projects. Fairbanks, Maslin, Maullin and Associates, "Opinion Research and Public Policy Analysis," *Resources for Youth*, March 1997.

12. Moore, Estrich, et al., *Dangerous Offenders* (Harvard, 1984).

13. Adam Walinsky, "A Nation in Chaos," *Atlanta Journal Constitution*, July 9, 1995, p. B1.

14. Jill Smolowe, "And Throw Away the Key," *Time*, February 7, 1994. Susan M. Collins, "Fighting Back against Youth Crime," *Bangor Daily News*, September 6, 1996. Morton Kondracke, "Crimewave, Coming Soon, Demands Action," *Commercial Appeal*, May 14, 1995, p. B4.

4. Honest Lawyers

1. Abraham Lincoln, "Notes for a Law Lecture," rpt. in *Great Sayings by Great Lawyers*, ed. G. J. Clark (1922), p. 432.
2. Connie J. A. Beck, Bruce D. Sales, and Andrew H. Benjamin, "Lawyer Distress: Alcohol-related Problems and Other Psychological Concerns among a Sample of Practicing Lawyers," 10 *Journal of Law and Health* 1 (1995).
3. William Simon, "The Ethics of Criminal Defense," 91 *Michigan Law Review* 173 (1993).
4. Harry I. Subin, "The Criminal Defense Lawyer's 'Different Mission': Reflections on the 'Right' to Present a False Case," 1 *Georgetown Journal of Legal Ethics*, 125 (1987).
5. Barbara A. Babcock, "Defending the Guilty," 32 *Cleveland State Law Review* 175 (1983–1984).
6. Floyd Abrams, "Why Lawyers Lie," *New York Times Magazine*, October 9, 1994.
7. "Photos Cast McVeigh in Different Light," Associated Press Wire, June 16, 1995. Josh Barbanel, "4 Lawyers in Lurid NY Shooting Case Showed Sensationalist Bent," *New York Times*, October 4, 1992.
8. Lorraine Hansberry, *A Raisin in the Sun* (Modern Library, 1995).
9. Oliver Wendell Holmes, "The Path of the Law after One Hundred Years," 110 *Harvard Law Review* 991 (1997).

Bibliography

Books

Abramson, Jeffrey. *We, the Jury: The Jury System and the Ideal of Democracy*. Basic Books, 1994.

Adler, Stephen J. *The Jury: Trial and Error in the American Courtroom*. Times Books, 1994.

Alexander, James. *A Brief Narrative of the Case and Trial of John Peter Zenger, Printer of the New York Weekly Journal*. Belknap Press of Harvard University Press, 1963.

Amar, Akhil. *The Constitution and Criminal Procedure: First Principles*. Yale, 1996.

American Law Institute. *Model Penal Code and Commentaries*. The American Law Institute, 1980–1985.

Anderson, David C. *Crime and the Politics of Hysteria: How the Willie Horton Story Changed American Justice*. Random House, 1995.

Apesperi, Eleni, and Geoffrey Albert. *The Role of Differential Experience with the Criminal Justice System in Changes in Perceptions of Severity of Legal Sanctions over Time*. National Council on Crime and Delinquency, 1993.

Arron, Deborah L. *The Alarming Growth of Dissatisfaction among Lawyers*. Berkeley: Ten Speed Press, 1991.

Baldwin, John, and Michael McConville. *Jury Trials*. Clarendon Press, 1979.

Bell, Derrick. *Confronting Authority: Reflections of an Ardent Protester*. Beacon Press, 1994.

————*Faces at the Bottom of the Well: The Permanence of Racism.* Basic Books, 1992.

————*And We Are Not Saved: The Elusive Quest for Racial Justice.* Basic Books, 1989.

————*Race, Racism and American Law.* Little, Brown, 1992.

Blumstein, Alfred, Jacqueline Cohen, et al. *Criminal Careers and "Career Criminals,"* vol. 1. National Research Council, National Academy Press, 1986.

Bochnak, Elizabeth. *Women's Self-Defense Cases: Theory and Practice.* Michie, 1981.

Calabresi, Guido, and Philip Bobbitt. *Tragic Choices.* Norton, 1978.

Chaiken, Jan. *Varieties of Criminal Behavior.* RAND Corporation, 1982.

Cover, Robert M., and Owen M. Fiss. *The Structure of Procedure.* Foundation Press, 1979.

Dershowitz, Alan M. *Reasonable Doubts: The O. J. Simpson Case and the Criminal Justice System.* Simon & Schuster, 1996.

————*The Abuse Excuse and Other Cop-outs, Sob Stories, and Evasions of Responsibility.* Little, Brown, 1994.

Dressler, Joshua. *Understanding Criminal Law.* Matthew Bender, 1987.

Dworkin, Ronald. *Law's Empire.* Harvard University Press, 1986.

Dzienkowski, John S. *Selected Statutes, Rules and Standards on the Legal Profession.* West Publishing, 1994.

Ewing, Charles Patrick. *Battered Women Who Kill: Psychological Self-Defense as Legal Justification.* Lexington Books, 1987.

Felony Arrests. Vera Institute of Justice, 1979.

Fletcher, George P. *With Justice for Some: Victim's Rights in Criminal Trials.* Addison-Wesley, 1995.

————*Rethinking Criminal Law.* Little, Brown, 1978.

————*A Crime of Self-Defense: Bernhard Goetz and the Law on Trial.* University of Chicago Press, 1988.

Fogel, David. *"We Are Living Proof": The Justice Model for Corrections.* W. H. Anderson, 1979.

Frankel, Marvin. *Criminal Sentences: Law without Order.* Hill and Wang, 1973.

Freedman, Monroe. *Lawyers' Ethics in an Adversary System.* Bobbs-Merrill Publishing, 1975.

Gillers, Stephen. *Regulation of Lawyers: Problems of Law and Ethics,* 3rd ed. Little, Brown, 1992.

Goodstein, Lynne, and John Hepburn. *Determinate Sentencing and Imprisonment: A Failure of Reform.* W. H. Anderson, 1985.

Greenwood, Peter W. *Diverting Children from a Life of Crime.* RAND Corporation, 1996.

——*Three Strikes and You're Out.* RAND Corporation, 1994.

——*Selective Incapacitation Revisited.* RAND Corporation, 1987.

Hans, Valerie P., and Neil Vidmar. *Judging the Jury.* Plenum Press, 1986.

Hart, Henry M., and Albert M. Sacks. *The Legal Process: Basic Problems in the Making and Application of Law.* Foundation Press, 1994.

Hart, H. L. A. *The Morality of the Criminal Law.* Oxford University Press, 1964.

——*Punishment and Responsibility.* Oxford University Press, 1968.

Hastie, Reid, et al. *Inside the Jury.* Harvard University Press, 1983.

Higginbotham, Leon, Jr. *In the Matter of Color: Race and the American Legal Process.* Oxford University Press, 1978.

Holmes, Oliver Wendell. *The Common Law.* Little, Brown, 1881.

Kadish, Mortimer R., and Sanford H. Kadish. *Discretion to Disobey.* Stanford University Press, 1973.

Kadish, Sanford H. *Encyclopedia of Crime and Justice,* vol. 1. Free Press, 1983.

Kalven, Harry, and Hans Zeisel. *The American Jury.* University of Chicago Press, 1966.

Kennedy, Duncan. *Legal Education and the Reproduction of Hierarchy: A Polemic against the System.* Afar Press, 1983.

Kennedy, Randall. *Race, Crime, and the Law.* Pantheon, 1996.

Kleiman, Mark A. R. *Against Excess.* Basic Books, 1992.

Kopel, David B. *Prison Blues: How America's Foolish Sentencing Policies Endanger Public Safety.* CATO Institute, 1994.

LaFave, Wayne R., and Austin W. Scott, Jr. *Criminal Law,* 2nd ed. West Publishing, 1986.

Levine, James P. *Juries and Politics.* Books/Cole Publishing, 1992.

Luban, David. *Lawyers and Justice: An Ethical Study.* Princeton University Press, 1988.

MacKinnon, Catharine A. *Feminism Unmodified: Discourses on Life and Law.* Harvard University Press, 1987.

Minow, Martha. *Making All the Difference: Inclusion, Exclusion and American Law.* Cornell University Press, 1990.

Moore, Mark, Susan Estrich, et al. *Dangerous Offenders: The Elusive Target of Justice.* Harvard University Press, 1984.

Moore, Michael. *Act and Crime: The Philosophy of Action and Its Implication for Criminal Law.* Oxford University Press, 1993.

———*Law and Psychiatry: Rethinking the Relationship.* Cambridge University Press, 1984.

Morris, Norvall. *Madness and the Criminal Law.* University of Chicago Press, 1982.

———*The Future of Imprisonment.* University of Chicago Press, 1974.

National Commission on Reform of Federal Criminal Laws. *Working Papers.* 1970.

Packer, Herbert. *The Limits of the Criminal Sanction.* Stanford University Press, 1968.

Piehl, Anne Morrison, and John J. DiIulio Jr. *Does Prison Pay Revisited.* Brookings Institute, 1995.

Posner, Richard. *The Problems of Jurisprudence.* Harvard University Press, 1990.

RAND Corporation. *California's New Three Strikes Law: Benefits, Costs, and Alternatives.* 1994.

———*Three Strikes Would Cut Crime But High Costs Make Full Effects Unlikely: Other Sentencing Options Could Achieve Crime Reductions at Less Cost.* 1994.

Rhode, Deborah L., and David Luban. *Legal Ethics.* Foundation Press, 1993.

Shane-DuBow, Sandra, et al. *Sentencing Reform in the United States: History, Content, and Effect.* U.S. Department of Justice, 1985.

Sherman, Lawrence W. *Policing Domestic Violence: Experiments and Dilemmas.* Free Press, 1992.

Silberman, Charles E. *Criminal Violence, Criminal Justice.* Random House, 1978.

Stone, Alan. *Law, Psychiatry, and Morality.* American Psychiatric Press, 1984.

Thaler, Paul. *The Watchful Eye: American Justice on the Television Trial.* Praeger, 1994.

Tonry, Michael. *Malign Neglect: Race, Crime, and Punishment in America.* Oxford University Press, 1995.

Tocqueville, Alexis de. *Democracy in America,* 13th ed., ed. J. P. Mayer, trans. George Lawrence. Doubleday, 1969.

Traver, Robert. *Anatomy of a Murder.* St. Martin's Press, 1958.

Van Dyke, John M. *Jury Selection Procedures.* Ballinger, 1977.

Von Hirsch, Andrew. *Doing Justice: The Choice of Punishments.* Hill and Wang, 1976.

Walker, Lenore E. *The Battered Woman.* Harper & Row, 1979.

Williams, Glanville. *Criminal Law: The General Part,* 2nd ed. Stevens, 1961.

Wilson, James Q. *Moral Judgment: Does the Abuse Excuse Threaten Our Legal System?* Basic Books, 1997.

———*Thinking about Crime.* Basic Books, 1975.

Wilson, James Q., and Richard Herrnstein. *Crime and Human Nature.* Simon & Schuster, 1985.

Wolfgang, Marvin, et al. *Delinquency in a Birth Cohort.* University of Chicago Press, 1972.

Zimring, Franklin E. *Perspectives on Deterrence.* U.S. Government Printing Office, 1971.

Zimring, Franklin E., and Gordon J. Hawkins. *Incapacitation: Penal Confinement and the Restraint of Crime.* Oxford University Press, 1995.

———*Deterrence: The Legal Threat in Crime Control.* University of Chicago Press, 1973.

Casebooks

Kadish, Sanford H., and Stephen J. Schulhofer. *Criminal Law and Its Processes,* 6th ed. Little, Brown, 1995.

Kaplan, John, and Robert Weisberg. *Criminal Law,* 2nd ed. Little, Brown, 1991.

Loewy, Arnold H. *Criminal Law.* W. H. Anderson, 1991.

Low, Peter, John Jeffries, et al. *Criminal Law: Cases and Materials,* 2nd ed. Foundation Press, 1986.

Rhode, Deborah L., and David Luban. *Legal Ethics.* Foundation Press, 1993.

Saltzburg, Stephen A., John L. Diamond, et al. *Criminal Law.* Michie, 1994.

Vorenberg, James. *Criminal Law and Procedure,* 2nd ed. West Publishing, 1981.

Weinreb, Lloyd L. *Leading Constitutional Cases on Criminal Justice.* Foundation Press, 1992.

Bibliography

Articles

PROLOGUE

Anderson, David. "The Crime Funnel." *New York Times Magazine,* June 12, 1994.

Kennedy, Duncan. "Form and Substance in Private Law Adjudication." 89 *Harvard Law Review* 1685 (1976).

McCarthy, Nancy. "9 Months of Testimony, 3 Hours of Deliberation and a Not Guilty Verdict Reveal a Public Divided Over Race and Justice." *California Bar Journal,* November 1995.

Puente, Maria. "Poll: Blacks' Confidence in Police Plummets." *USA Today,* March 21, 1995.

Wells, Catherine. "Tort Law as Corrective Justice: A Pragmatic Justification for Jury Adjudication." 88 *Michigan Law Review* 2348 (1990).

1. POLITICS AND THE REASONABLE MAN

Angel, Marina. "Criminal Law and Women: Giving the Abused Woman Who Kills a Jury of Her Peers Who Appreciate Trifles." 33 *American Criminal Law Review* 230 (1996).

Arenella, Peter. "The Diminished Capacity and Diminished Responsibility Defenses: Two Children of a Doomed Marriage." 77 *Columbia Law Review* 827 (1977).

Bartlett, Katherine T. "Feminist Legal Methods." 103 *Harvard Law Review* 829 (1990).

Bazelon, David L. "The Morality of the Criminal Law." 49 *Southern California Law Review* 385 (1976).

Carrillo, Luis A. "How To Kill a Latino Kid and Walk Free." *Los Angeles Times,* November 27, 1995.

Cekola, Anna."Tragic Death Left Scar on San Clemente." *Los Angeles Times,* March 4, 1994.

Coker, Donna K. "Heat of Passion and Wife Killing: Men Who Batter/ Men Who Kill." 2 *Southern California Review of Law & Women's Studies* 72 (1992).

Coughlin, Anne M. "Excusing Women." 82 *California Law Review* 1 (1994).

Donavan, Dolores A., and Stephanie M. Wildman. "Is the Reasonable Man Obsolete? A Critical Perspective on Self-Defense and Provocation." 14 *Loyola Los Angeles Law Review* 435 (1981).

Durham, Alexis M., III. "Justice in Sentencing: The Role of Prior Record of Criminal Involvement." 78 *Journal of Criminal Law & Criminology* 614 (1987).

Fletcher, George P. "The Individualization of Excusing Conditions." 47 *Southern California Law Review* 1269 (1974).

Hoffman, Jan. "Defending Men Who Kill Their Loved Ones." *New York Times,* July 10, 1994.

Johnson, Kevin. "Insanity Defense a Tough Strategy, Law Experts Say." *Los Angeles Times,* May 11, 1993.

Littleton, Christine A. "Reconstructing Sexual Equality." 75 *California Law Review* 1279 (1987).

Maguian, Holly. "Battered Women and Self Defense: Myths and Misconceptions in Current Reform Proposals." 140 *University of Pennsylvania Law Review* 379 (1991).

Meyer, Josh. "Slaying of Tagger Strikes Deep Chord in Community." *Los Angeles Times,* February 5, 1995.

Michel, Chuck. "The Real Victims Are the Gun Owners of L.A." *Los Angeles Times,* November 27, 1995.

Morse, Stephen J. "Undiminished Confusion in Diminished Capacity." 75 *Journal of Criminal Law & Criminology* 1 (1984).

Osthoff, Sue. "Making a Difference: Advocating Effectively for Women Who Kill." Philadelphia: National Clearinghouse for the Defense of Battered Women, 1992.

Quan, Doris. "Relatives Try to Rally Support for Boys Who Killed Father, Man Described as Bully; Lawyers Plan Battered Child Defense." *Dallas Morning News,* August 18, 1993.

Robinson, Paul H. "Criminal Law Defenses: A Systematic Analysis." 82 *Columbia Law Review* 199 (1982).

Schneider, Elizabeth M. "Particularity and Generality: Challenges of Feminist Theory and Practices in Work on Woman-Abuse," 67 *New York University Law Review* 520 (1992).

——"Describing and Changing: Women's Self-Defense Work and the Problem of Expert Testimony on Battering." 9 *Women's Rights Legal Report* 195 (1986).

Silberman, Charles E. "Truth and Justice: Why the Best Hope in a 'War' on Crime May Be a Stalemate." *New York Times,* January 30, 1994.

Spatz, Melissa. "A 'Lesser' Crime: A Comparative Study of Legal Defenses for Men Who Kill Their Wives." 24 *Columbia Journal of Law & Societal Problems* 597 (1991).

Tulsky, Fredric N., and Ted Rohrlich. "And Justice for Some: Solving Murders in LA County." *Los Angeles Times,* December 1, 1996.

Weinstein, Jeremy D. "Adultery, Law, and the State: A History." 33 *Hastings Law Journal* 195 (1986).

Williams, Glanville. "Provocation and the Reasonable Man." 1954 *Criminal Law Review* 740.

Williams, Wendy. "The Equality Crisis: Some Reflections on Culture, Courts, and Feminism." 7 *Women's Rights Law Reporter* 175 (1982).

2. SEND THEM A MESSAGE

"Acquittal in Doorstep Killing of Japanese Student." *New York Times,* May 24, 1993.

Alschuler, Albert W. "The Supreme Court and the Jury: Voir Dire, Peremptory Challenges, and the Review of Jury Verdicts." 56 *University of Chicago Law Review* 153 (1989).

Amar, Akhil R. "The Bill of Rights as a Constitution." 100 *Yale Law Journal* 1131 (1991).

Amegashie, Kajo. "Blacks Must Try to Bridge Gap with the Police." *Star Tribune Newspaper of the Twin Cities,* July 3, 1996.

Austin, Regina. "The Black Community, Its Law Breakers and a Politics of Identification." 65 *Southern California Law Review* 1769 (1992).

Babcock, Barbara. "Voir Dire: Preserving 'Its Wonderful Power.'" 27 *Stanford Law Review* 545 (1975).

Butler, Paul. "Racially Based Jury Nullification: Black Power in the Criminal Justice System." 105 *Yale Law Journal* 167 (1995).

——— "Black Jurors: Right to Acquit? Jury Nullification." *Harper's Magazine,* December 1995.

Cain, Patricia A. "Feminist Jurisprudence: Grounding the Theories." 4 *Berkeley Women's Law Journal* 191 (1989/1990).

Carter, Stephen. "When Victims Happen to Be Black." 97 *Yale Law Journal* 420 (1988).

Dolan, Maura. "Why Jurors Err: They're Just Human." *Los Angeles Times,* September 25, 1994.

"Drug Prosecutions Are Biased, Some Minorities Say; Problem Is 'Among Inner-City Street Gangs, Not Suburban Bowling Leagues,' Retorts Official." *St. Louis Post-Dispatch,* May 19, 1996.

Gates, Henry L., Jr. "Thirteen Ways of Looking at a Black Man." *New Yorker,* October 23, 1995.

Howe, Mark DeWolfe. "Juries as Judges of Criminal Law." 52 *Harvard Law Review* 582 (1939).

Johnson, Phillip E. "Book Review." 50 *University of Chicago Law Review* 1534 (1983).

Kennedy, Randall. "The State, Criminal Law, and Racial Discrimination: A Comment." 107 *Harvard Law Review* 1255 (1994).

Kotler, Martin A. "Reappraising the Jury's Role as Finder of Fact." 20 *Georgia Law Review* 123 (1985).

Marder, Nancy S. "Beyond Gender: Peremptory Challenges and the Roles of the Jury." 73 *Texas Law Review* 1041 (1995).

———"Gender Dynamics and Jury Deliberations." 96 *Yale Law Journal* 593 (1987).

Patterson, Orlando. "The Paradox of Integration." *New Republic,* November 6, 1995, p. 24.

Resnik, Judith. "Ninth Circuit Gender Bias Task Force, The Effects of Gender in the Federal Courts." 67 *Southern California Law Review* 745 (1993).

Roberts, Dorothy E. "Punishing Drug Addicts Who Have Babies: Women of Color, Equality, and the Right of Privacy." 104 *Harvard Law Review* 1419 (1991).

Russell, Katheryn K. "A Critical View from the Inside: An Application of Critical Legal Studies to Criminal Law." 85 *Journal of Criminal Law & Criminology* 222 (1993).

Sanchez, Rene. "Black College Enrollment Shows Increase: Overall Rate for African-Americans Still Behind, Study Finds." *Washington Post,* December 12, 1994.

Stevens, John Paul. "The Freedom of Speech." 102 *Yale Law Journal* 1293 (1993).

Walinsky, Adam. "The Crisis of Public Order." *Atlantic Monthly*, July 1995.

Weisbrod, Carol. "Images of the Woman Juror." 9 *Harvard Women's Law Journal* 59 (1986).

Wells, Catherine P. "Tort Law as Corrective Justice: A Pragmatic Justification for Jury Adjudication." 88 *Michigan Law Review* 2348 (1990).

Wilson, J. Q., and George Kelling. "Broken Windows." *Atlantic Monthly*, March 1982.

Zeisel, Hans, and Shari S. Diamond. "The Effect of Peremptory Challenges on Jury and Verdict: An Experiment in a Federal District Court." 30 *Stanford Law Review* 491 (1978).

3. THE LONG SHADOW OF WILLIE HORTON

Abrahamson, Alan. "Chat Sessions Weigh Fates of Three-Strikes Defendants Courts: Senior Prosecutors Grapple with 'Trying to Do the Right Thing' at Weekly, Informal Discussions." *Los Angeles Times*, July 2, 1996 (part of a three-part series).

———"Judicial Panel Seeks Repeal of Mandatory Sentence Law." *Los Angeles Times*, January 29, 1990.

Alexander, Elizabeth. "The New Turn of the Screw: Why Good News about Controlling Incarceration Rates Safely May Not Be Welcome." 66 *Southern California Law Review* 209 (1992).

Berkman, Harvey. "Court to Take on Sentencing Rule." *The National Law Journal*, January 15, 1996.

Bray, Dwayne. "Theft Case at Center of '3 Strikes' Controversy." *Los Angeles Times*, July 18, 1994.

Clarke, Judy. "The Sentencing Guidelines: What a Mess." *Federal Probation*, December 1991.

DiIulio, John J., Jr. "Moral Poverty: The Coming of the Super-Predators Should Scare Us into Wanting to Get to the Root Causes of Crime a Lot Faster." *Chicago Tribune*, December 15, 1995.

Dolan, Maura, and Tony Perry. "Justices Deal Blow to '3 Strikes' Lower Courts Allowed Discretion in Sentencing." *Los Angeles Times*, June 21, 1996.

Durham, Alexis M., III. "Public Opinion Regarding Sentences for Crime: Does It Exist?" 21 *Journal of Criminal Justice* 1 (1993).

Eisele, Thomas. "The Sentencing Guidelines: Two Views from the

Bench." 55 *Journal of Correctional Philosophy and Practice* 16 (1991).

Fox, James Alan. "Prepared Statement of James Alan Fox, Dean of the College of Criminal Justice, Northeastern University, before the Senate Judiciary Committee, Subcommittee on Youth Violence, Hearings on the Impending Youth Crime Wave." *Federal News Service,* February 28, 1996.

Freed, Daniel J. "Federal Sentencing in the Wake of the Guidelines: Unacceptable Limits on the Discretion of Sentences." 28 *American Criminal Law Review* 161 (1991).

Geis, Gilbert. "Our System of Punishment Doesn't Work." *Los Angeles Times,* August 1, 1994.

Hatch, Orrin G. "The Role of Congress in Sentencing: The United States Sentencing Commission, Mandatory Minimum Sentences, and the Search for a Certain and Effective Sentencing System." 28 *Wake Forest Law Review* 188 (1993).

King, Peter H. "On California: All Aboard the Crime Bandwagon." *Los Angeles Times,* January 9, 1994.

Krikorian, Greg. "Front-Line Fights over 3 Strikes: Angry Voters Sent a Simple Message—Get Tough on Repeat Offenders." *Los Angeles Times,* July 1, 1996.

———"More Blacks Imprisoned under '3 Strikes,' Study Says." *Los Angeles Times,* March 5, 1996.

Lay, Donald P. "Rethinking the Guidelines: A Call for Cooperation." 101 *Yale Law Journal* 1755 (1992).

Lowenthal, Gary T. "Mandatory Sentencing Laws: Undermining the Effectiveness of Determinate Sentencing Reform." 81 *California Law Review* 61 (1993).

Maharaj, Davan. "8% of Orange County Delinquents Linked to 55% of Repeat Crimes." *Los Angeles Times,* September 28, 1993.

Morse, Stephen J. "Blame and Danger: An Essay on Preventive Detention." 76 *Boston University Law Review* 113 (1996).

Nagel, Ilene H. "Structuring Sentencing Discretion: The New Federal Sentencing Guidelines." 80 *Journal of Criminal Law & Criminology* 883 (1990).

Ostrow, Ronald J. "Los Angeles Times Interview: Philip Heymann; A Veteran of Five Justice Departments Reflects on His Bosses." *Los Angeles Times,* February 20, 1994.

Pringle, Peter. "Clinton Crime Bill Is a Sham, Say Critics." *The Independent,* March 10, 1994.

Rivera, Carla. "Study Finds Aid Outdoes '3 Strikes' in Crime Fight." *Los Angeles Times,* June 20, 1996.

Robinson, Paul H. "A Sentencing System for the 21st Century?" 66 *Texas Law Review* 1 (1987).

Sharkey, Katherine M. "Out of Sight, Out of Mind: Is Blind Faith in Incapacitation Justified?" 105 *Yale Law Journal* 1433 (1996).

Simon, Jonathan. "Crime and Punishment—And Politics." *Los Angeles Times,* January 17, 1994.

Simon, Stephanie. "Backers of Three Strikes Unflinchingly Defend Law." *Los Angeles Times,* July 3, 1996.

Skelton, George. "Capitol Journal: A Father's Crusade Born from Pain." *Los Angeles Times,* December 9, 1993.

Skolnick, Jerome H. "Perspective on Imprisonment." *Los Angeles Times,* December 16, 1993.

———"Swamping the System with Small Fish." *Los Angeles Times,* June 27, 1996.

Smolowe, Jill. "And Throw Away the Key." *Time,* February 7, 1994.

Stith, Kate, and Steve Koh. "The Politics of Sentencing Reform." 28 *Wake Forest Law Review* 223 (1993).

Taylor, Stuart, Jr. "How Racist Drug War Swells Violent Crime." *American Lawyer,* April 1993.

Tjoflat, Gerald Bard. "The Untapped Potential for Judicial Decision under the Federal Sentencing Guidelines: Advice for Counsel." 55 *Journal of Correctional Philosophy and Practice* 4 (1991).

Wilkins, William W., Jr. "The United States Sentencing Commission: Its Many Missions." 55 *Journal of Correctional Philosophy and Practice* 26 (1991).

Zeno, Thomas E. "A Prosecutor's View of the Sentencing Guidelines." 55 *Journal of Correctional Philosophy and Practice* 31 (1991).

4. HONEST LAWYERS

Abrams, Floyd. "Why Lawyers Lie." *New York Times,* October 9, 1994.

Babcock, Barbara A. "Defending the Guilty." 32 *Cleveland State Law Review* 175 (1983–1984).

Berkowitz-Caballero, Esther. "In the Aftermath of Gentile: Reconsidering the Efficacy of Trial Publicity Rules." 68 *New York University Law Review* 494 (1993).

Chanen, Jill. "Lawyers Finding Satisfaction in Getting Out or Scaling Down." *Chicago Lawyer,* March 1994.

Cook, Alberta I. "Lawyers Lured by Other Careers, Lifestyles." *National Law Journal,* February 16, 1987.

Dolan, Maura. "Jury System Is Held in Low Regard by Most." *Los Angeles Times,* September 27, 1994.

Dyer, Carolyn S., and Nancy R. Hauserman. "Electronic Coverage of the Courts: Exceptions to Exposure." 75 *Georgetown Law Journal* 1633 (1987).

Frankel, Marvin. "The Search for Truth: An Umpireal View." 123 *University of Pennsylvania Law Review* 1031 (1975).

Fried, Charles. "The Lawyer as Friend: The Moral Foundations of the Lawyer-Client Relation." 85 *Yale Law Journal* 1060 (1976).

Hazard, Geoffrey C., Jr. "The Lawyer's Obligation to Be Trustworthy When Dealing with Opposing Parties." 33 *Southern California Law Review* 181 (1981).

Luban, David. "Are Criminal Defenders Different?" 91 *Michigan Law Review* 1729 (1993).

———"Commentary: Partisanship, Betrayal, and Autonomy in the Lawyer-Client Relation: A Reply to Stephen Ellmann." 90 *Columbia Law Review* 1004 (1990).

———"Paternalism and the Legal Profession." 1981 *Wisconsin Law Review* 454 (1981).

McCarthy, Nancy. "Judicial Evaluation Process Assailed over Rating of Brown." *California Bar Journal,* June 1996.

———"The Fallout." *California Bar Journal,* November 1995.

Mitchell, John B. "Reasonable Doubts Are Where You Find Them: A Response to Professor Subin's Position on the Criminal Lawyer's 'Different Mission.'" 1 *Georgetown Journal of Legal Ethics* 339 (1987).

———"The Ethics of the Criminal Defense Attorney—New Answers to Old Questions." 32 *Stanford Law Review* 292 (1980).

Moses, Jonathan M. "Legal Spin Control: Ethics and Advocacy in the Court of Public Opinion." 95 *Columbia Law Review* 1811 (1995).

Ogletree, Charles, Jr. "Beyond Justifications: Seeking Motivations to Sustain Public Defenders." 106 *Harvard Law Review* 1239 (1993).

Orey, Michael. "Legions of Lawyers—Including Partners at Top Firms—Are Unhappy with Their Jobs. What Is the Cause of This Discontent? And Is There a Cure?" *American Lawyer,* October 1993.

Resnik, Judith. "Asking about Gender in Courts." 21 *Signs: Journal of Women in Culture and Society* 952 (1996).

Rhode, Deborah. "Ethical Perspectives on Legal Practice." 37 *Stanford Law Review* 589 (1985).

———"Moral Character as a Professional Credential." 96 *Yale Law Journal* 481 (1985).

———"Perspectives on Professional Women." 40 *Stanford Law Review* 1163 (1988).

Scardino, Albert. "Courtroom TV Is a Fixture, Even as New York Is Deciding." *New York Times,* January 22, 1989.

Simon, William H. "Ethical Discretion in Lawyering." 101 *Harvard Law Review* 1083 (1988).

———"The Ethics of Criminal Defense." 91 *Michigan Law Review* 1703 (1993).

Subin, Harry I. "The Criminal Defense Lawyer's 'Different Mission': Reflections on the 'Right' to Present a False Case." 1 *Georgetown Journal of Legal Ethics* 125 (1987).

———"Is This Lie Necessary? Further Reflections on the Right to Present a False Defense." 1 *Georgetown Journal of Legal Ethics* 689 (1988).

———"The Lawyers as Superego: Disclosure of Client Confidences to Prevent Harm." 70 *Iowa Law Review* 1091 (1985).

Wieder, Robert S. "How to Manipulate the Media." *California Lawyer,* February 1994.

EPILOGUE

Fairbanks, Maslin, Maullin and Associates. "Opinion Research and Public Policy Analysis." *Resources for Youth,* March 1997.

Nourse, Victoria. "Passion's Progress: Modern Law Reform and the Provocation Defense." 106 *Yale Law Journal* 1331 (1997).

Tulsky, Fredric, and Ted Rohrlich. "And Justice for Some: Solving Murders in LA County." *Los Angeles Times,* December 1, 1996.

Cases

Ake v. Oklahoma, 470 U.S. 68 (1985), holding that a state must provide defense with a psychiatrist when the defendant's sanity is at issue.

Allison v. State, 86 S.W. 409 Ark. (1904), holding that the doctrine of imperfect self-defense applies when the defendant possesses a negligently formed but honest belief in the need to use force in self-defense.

Baker v. Carr, 369 U.S. 186 (1962), holding that the Constitution requires equal representation.

Ballard v. United States, 329 U.S. 187 (1946), holding that the exclusion of women from a jury could be highly prejudicial to a defendant.

Barnes et al. v. Commonwealth of Virginia, 190 Va. 732 (1950), holding that a jury should not be swayed by "passion, prejudice or sympathy" in rendering its decision.

Batson v. Kentucky, 476 U.S. 79 (1986), prohibiting race-based exercise of peremptory challenges.

Bedder v. Director of Public Prosecutions, All. E. 805 (1954), holding that the "reasonable man standard" does not include impotence.

Berger v. United States, 295 U.S. 78 (1935), holding that a prosecutor may "strike hard blows but he is not at liberty to strike foul ones. It is as much his duty to refrain from improper methods calculated to produce a wrongful conviction as it is to use every legitimate means to bring about a just one."

Brady v. Maryland, 373 U.S. 83 (1963), mandating that prosecutors share potentially exculpatory information with an accused, although there is no mirror obligation.

Brown v. Board of Education, 347 U.S. 483 (1954), holding that segregation of public schools is unconstitutional.

California v. Brown, 479 U.S. 538 (1987), affirming death sentence following instruction that jury should not be influenced by "mere sentiment, conjecture, sympathy, passion, prejudice, public opinion or public feeling."

Chicago Council of Lawyers v. Bauer et al., 522 F.2d 242 7th Cir. (1975), striking down the "over broad" ABA standard, which restricted attorneys' comments about pending litigation. The court proposed judges proscribe only those comments that posed a "serious and imminent threat" to the fair administration of justice.

Commonwealth v. Kendrick, 218 N.E.2d 408 Mass. (1966), holding that an act of self-defense when excessive shifts culpability from the attacker to the victim.

Commonwealth v. Martin, 369 Mass. 640 (1976), holding that the justification for defense of a third party does not stop at the prison gates.

Commonwealth v. Whitler, 2 Brewster 388 Pa. Ct. Of Oyer & Terminer (1868), holding that circumstances surrounding crimes of passion are unique and therefore deserve mitigation.

Crawford v. State, 190 A.2d 538 Md. (1963), holding that a necessity instruction is required where the defendant was shot, then shot the victim after hearing footsteps behind him.

Duncan v. Louisiana, 391 U.S. 145 (1968), applying fair trial guarantee to the states.

Durham v. United States, 214 F.2d 862 D.C. (1954), holding that a defendant is not criminally responsible if the unlawful act was the product of a mental disease or defect.

Edmonson v. Leesville Concrete Co., 500 U.S. 614 (1991), finding that there is state action where private lawyers in civil cases use litigation procedures to exclude black jurors.

Freddo v. State, 155 S.W. 170 Tenn. (1913), holding that circumstances which mitigate murder to manslaughter must be such that the provocation would be resented by an average reasonable man.

Geders v. United States, 425 U.S. 80 (1976), holding that if our "adversary system is to function according to design we must assume that an attorney will observe his responsibilities to the legal system, as well as to his client."

Gentile v. Nevada, 501 U.S. 1030 (1991), holding that states can sanction an attorney for making extrajudicial statements which will have a "substantial likelihood of materially prejudicing an adjudicative proceeding."

Gideon v. Wainwright, 372 U.S. 335 (1963), holding that a fair trial may not be assured without the assistance of counsel.

Hernandez v. New York, 500 U.S. 352 (1991), rejecting showing of a pattern of race-based disparities as sufficient to trigger reversal; requiring specific proof.

Hill v. State, 118 Miss. 170 (1918), holding that in self-defense cases the "reasonable person" is of the same size and strength as the defendant.

Holmes v. Director of Public Prosecutors, 2 All E.R. 124 (1946), holding that a defense which successfully meets all the elements of provocation reduces a charge of murder to manslaughter.

Hoyt v. Florida, 368 U.S. 57 (1975), holding that a woman's status as the center of the home and family life made it reasonable for a state to exempt women from mandatory jury service.

Ibn Tamas v. United States, 407 A.2d 626 (1979), holding expert testimony of BWS relevant to enhance defendant credibility and support her testimony that she feared imminent danger is admissible to determine state of mind.

In Re Christian S., 7 Cal. 4th 768 (1994), holding that the statutory elimination of the diminished capacity defense does not eliminate the doctrine of imperfect self-defense.

J.E.B. v. Alabama ex rel. T.B., 511 U.S. 127 (1994), proscribing gender-based peremptory challenges because the discrimination serves to "ratify and perpetuate invidious, archaic, and over broad stereotypes about the relative abilities of men and women."

Johnson v. Oklahoma, 484 U.S. 878 (1987), holding that a jury should not be influenced by "sympathy, sentiment or prejudice" when imposing a sentence on a defendant.

Mapp v. Ohio, 367 U.S. 643 (1961), extending the exclusionary rule to the states.

M'Naughten Case, 8 Eng. Rep. 718 (1843), holding that an accused is not criminally responsible if he was unaware of the nature and quality of the act.

People v. Aphaylath, 502 N.E.2d 998 N.Y. (1986), holding that evidence of emotional disturbance brought on by feelings of isolation of a person in an alien culture is admissible.

People v. Berry, 556 P.2d 777 Cal. (1976), holding that husband's claim that wife's taunting about her love for another man and plan to leave him provoked him to strangle her can be admitted.

People v. Borchers, 325 P.2d 97 Cal. (1958), defining passion as any "violent, intense, high-wrought, or enthusiastic emotion."

People v. Ceballos, 12 Cal.3d 470 Cal. (1974), holding that a defendant is not warranted in using deadly force to protect property.

People v. Chen, Indictment No. 7774/87 N.Y. Sup. Ct. (1987), holding that cultural background affected defendant's mental state and made it impossible for him to form the requisite intent for murder.

People v. Chevalier, 544 N.E.2d Ill. (1989), holding that mere words are insufficient provocation . . . no matter how "aggravated, abusive or indecent the language."

People v. Croy, 41 Cal.3d 1 (1985), allowing cultural background defense as exculpatory evidence for defendant's murder conviction.

People v. Flannel, 25 Cal.3d 668 (1979), holding that the existence of an honest but unreasonable belief in the need for self-defense is inconsistent with murder.

People v. Goetz, 73 N.Y.2d 751 (1988), holding that the reasonableness standard must be based on the circumstances facing a defendant in his or her situation.

People v. Guenther, 740 P.2d 971 Col. (1987), holding that homeowner may use appropriate force to repel unauthorized person from entering into his home.

People v. Kimura, Los Angeles Sup. Ct. (1985), Japanese mother charged only with involuntary manslaughter in death of her two children based on considerations of Japanese culture.

People v. Kong Moua, Case No. 315972–0 Fresno Sup. Ct. (1985), stressing the importance of a coherent judicial policy regarding cases involving cultural conflict.

People v. Schmidt, 110 N.E. 945 (1915), holding that "a delusion that God himself has issued a command" has an effect in obscuring moral distinctions.

People v. Superior Court (Romero) 917 P.2d 628 Cal. (1996), holding that state judges retain discretion in sentencing under the three strikes law.

People v. Thompkins, 195 Cal.App.3d 244 (1987), holding that instructions stating that sudden heat of passion could not nullify premeditation is inadequate.

People v. Williams, 205 N.E.2d 749 Ill. (1965), holding that the trier of fact must consider whether an imminent threat is posed and whether the aggressor is willing and able to injure the defendant.

People v. Wu, 235 Cal.App.3d 614 (1991), holding that defendant's cultural background could be considered as relevant to state of mind when deciding guilt or innocence of defendant accused of murder.

Peters v. Kiff, 407 U.S. 493 (1972), holding that due process is denied by discriminatory jury selection.

Polk County v. Dodson, 454 U.S. 312 (1981), holding that although a defense attorney has a "duty to advance all colorable claims and defenses, the canons of professional ethics impose limits on permissible advocacy. It is the obligation of any lawyer . . . not to clog the courts with frivolous motions or appeals."

Powers v. Ohio, 499 U.S. 400 (1991), characterizing jury service as a "duty, honor and privilege"; holding that peremptory challenges cannot be used to exclude jurors not of the same race as defendant.

Reed v. State, 59 S.W.2d. 122 TX. (1933), holding that wife killing husband's lover is not within the scope of statute that makes homicide justifiable when husband kills his wife's lover.

Regina v. Ly, 33 Can. Crim. Cases (1987), excluding cultural background evidence, resulting in defendant's murder conviction.

Regina v. Morgan, A.C. 182 (1976), holding that defendants' unreasonable mistake about victim's consent in rape case negates requisite element of intent.

Robinson v. California, 370 U.S. 660 (1962), holding that due process requires an "act" as a basis of punishment.

Rowland v. State, 83 Miss. 483 (1904), holding that it is manslaughter when a husband, upon discovery of his wife committing adultery with a lover, shot at the lover and killed the wife.

Scroggs v. State, 93 S.E.2d 583 Ga. (1956), holding that wife killing to prevent adultery is justified but were she to kill in the heat of passion upon discovering commission of husband's adultery she would be guilty of manslaughter.

Shorter v. People, 2 N.Y. 193 (1849), holding that the defendant must have believed deadly force was necessary and a reasonable person in the same circumstances would have reacted the same way.

Sparf & Hansen v. United States, 156 U.S. 51 (1895), holding that jury's duty is to apply the law, as stated by the court, to the facts of the particular case.

State v. Abbott, 174 A.2d 881 N.J. (1961), holding that use of deadly force is not justified if "the actor knows that he can avoid the necessity of using such force with complete safety by retreating."

State v. Elliot, 411 A.2d. 3 Conn. (1979), setting forth the leading definition of extreme emotional disturbance.

State v. Kelly, 478 A.2d 364 N.J. (1984), holding that evidence of battered woman's syndrome is admissible.

State v. Kidd, 175 P.Rpt. 772 N.M. (1918), holding that although killing was not self-defense, there was sufficient provocation of fear to mitigate murder to voluntary manslaughter.

State v. Leidholm, 334 N.W.2d 811 N.D. (1983), concluding that learned helplessness is a manifestation of battered woman's syndrome which is admissible as to the defendant's perception of imminent bodily danger.

State v. Mayberry, 226 S.W.2d 725 Mo. (1950), holding that emotional disturbance might not justify the homicide, but may reduce the grade of the offense.

State v. Nelson, 329 N.W.2d 643 Io. (1983), holding that the use of force in defense of property is not justifiable if the crime happened earlier, away from the defendant.

State v. Ott, 686 P.2d 1001 Or. (1984), questioning whether extreme emotional disturbance may mitigate murder to manslaughter.

State v. Peacock, Md. Cir. Ct. Oct. 17, #94-CR-0943 (1994), sentencing a jealous husband to 18 months in prison for killing his wife after an argument.

State v. Wanrow, 601 P.2d 917 (1979), holding that self-defense instructions must afford women the right to have their conduct judged in light of physical differences in size and strength.

Strickland v. State, 257 Ga. 230 (1987), holding that a jury could find a defendant guilty of murder who shot his wife after she rejected a proposed reconciliation.

Swain v. Alabama, 380 U.S. 202 (1965), upholding race-based peremptory challenges.

United States v. Carolene Products, 304 U.S. 144 (1938), noting that federal courts provide additional protection for "discrete and insular minorities" from actions of political majority.

United States v. Dougherty, 473 F.2d 1113 (1972), warning of the dangers of setting no boundaries on jury decisions.

United States v. Thomas, 116 F.3d (2d Cir. 1997) (Cabranes, J.), emphasizing the dangers of jury nullification and the duty of juries to enforce the law.

United States v. Wade, 388 U.S. 218 (1967), holding that defense counsel has no obligation to "ascertain or present the truth . . . our interest in not convicting the innocent permits counsel to put the State to its proof, to put the State's case in the worst possible light, regardless of what he thinks or knows is the truth."

Vollbaum v. Texas, 833 S.W.2d 652 (1992), stating that homicide is punishable only when the conduct is voluntary and the accused has the culpable mental state.

Index